# To See Oursels...

O wad some Power the giftie gie us
To see oursels as ithers see us!

From "To a Louse"
by Robert Burns

# To See Oursels...

### Visitors to
### Dumfries and Galloway
### from medieval to modern times

A. E. MacRobert

Dumfries and Galloway
Libraries, Information and Archives
2001

Design, set and print by Solway Offset Services Limited, Dumfries for the publisher, Dumfries and Galloway Libraries, Information and Archives.

ISBN 0 946280 52 5

Dumfries and Galloway Libraries, Information and Archives
Central Support Unit, Catherine Street
Dumfries DG1 1JB

We also publish -

## Dumfries and Galloway: *Through the Lens*

The titles above are available through local libraries or any good bookshop, priced £2.50 or £3.50 per title including postage and packing from the above address.

A complete list of our publications is available from the above address or on our website at www.dumgal.go.uk/lia

# PREFACE

I wish to record my appreciation of help from the Kirkcudbright Library and Glasgow University Library, the National Library of Scotland and the British Library.

I also wish to thank my brother, Mr. T. M. MacRobert, for suggesting that I should compile this book. Thanks are also due to Lady Stewartby on behalf of the Buchan Trust for permission to use the extract from *Memory-Hold-the-Door*.

The spelling in some of the accounts has been modernised in order to facilitate understanding of some of them. Readers, however, may still find difficulties – especially in the earlier accounts with the word order, punctuation and grammar, which have not been altered. There are limits to the process of editing without altering the sense and feeling of the original.

References to the notes provided at the end of most of the accounts are shown by numbers within brackets in the text.

I especially wish to thank the Dumfries and Galloway Libraries, Information and Archives for steering the book through the printing and publishing processes and for selecting the interesting and apposite illustrations.

A.E.M.

# CONTENTS

# INTRODUCTION

The south-west of Scotland comprising Dumfries and Galloway has always been a very distinct part of Scotland in several ways. Geographically it is separated from the rest of the lowlands by ranges of high hills. Historically Galloway maintained a degree of independence from the Scottish Kings until the 12th century. Economically it has remained basically rural and agricultural without suffering some of the intense problems of the industrial belt in the centre of Scotland. There is no other part of Scotland with such varied and beautiful scenery. Between the Rhinns of Galloway in the west and the hills beyond Moffat and Langholm in the east there are mountains and moors, cliffs and beaches, islands and estuaries, rivers and lochs, forests and glens and green pastures.

This book provides descriptions of Dumfries and Galloway only by visitors. It therefore excludes accounts of writers such as Andrew Symson in the 17th century, Robert Heron in the 18th century, S.R.Crockett in the 19th, and C.H.Dick in the 20th century. So it may be similar to seeing through only one lens in a pair of spectacles. It could be argued that residents are the best people to appraise a particular area, but the impressions of visitors have also their own particular significance. Perhaps they have the benefit of a wider perspective. As Robert Burns wrote:

> 'O wad some Power the giftie gie us
> to see oursels as ithers see us!
> It wad frae mony a blunder free us,
> And foolish notion.'

It should not, however, be asserted that visitors are completely impartial, as they have an in-built bias, favourable or otherwise. Some of the English travellers, whose accounts have been included, clearly came to Scotland expecting lower standards of comfort and civilisation than in England. Some were pleasantly surprised! The reactions of certain travellers were also obviously affected by the poor conditions of the roads and the quality of the meals and accommodation which they encountered. Some of their more cantankerous and perhaps over-hasty comments have therefore been omitted.

It is inevitable that most of the accounts were written by well-known people who have left books and diaries for posterity. There have, of course, been countless who have left no record of their travels. It would be fascinating to have descriptions from a Roman soldier guarding the fortlet at Gatehouse of Fleet or Durisdeer; an attendant of James IV on a pilgrimage to Whithorn; and a Jacobite clansman passing through Dumfries in 1745.

There are tantalising gaps in what might have been available. Ben Jonson, the English dramatist (who thought his grandfather came from Annandale) visited Scotland in 1610, but any record of his impressions may have been destroyed in a fire a few years later in his lodgings. Dr Samuel Johnson in his visit to Scotland in 1773 did not proceed south of Auchinleck in Ayrshire, and the south-west was spared his dogmatic and pretentious comments. R.L.Stevenson went on a walking holiday in Wigtownshire in 1876 but left no record of it.

No selection of descriptions can be complete, and there are historical gaps which regrettably cannot be filled. The selection provided in this book nevertheless offers a wide panorama over several centuries. It should, however, be kept in mind that these travellers recorded only what they themselves saw or heard and found interesting. Their omissions are therefore almost as worthy of note. What would have been significant to us with our hindsight may not have seemed worthy of mention at the time. More information on schools and medical care would have been especially welcome.

Two particular themes stand out in many of the accounts. The first is the considerable difficulty in travelling until there were significant improvements during the 19th century. Roads were often just muddy tracks. There was no bridge at the mouth of the River Esk, and travellers had to ford the Solway sands - a crossing which could be fatal to those heedless of tide and wind. Routes into Nithsdale over the Lowther Hills and into Annandale down Ericstane Brae were notorious. Along the coast there were few good harbours partly due to the sands in the estuaries.

The second is the poverty of most people during centuries of virtual stagnation in living conditions until a remarkable transformation gathered momentum during the second half of the 18th century. The earlier accounts which portray the low standards of living are not palatable reading, but they have to be seen together with the later accounts showing the changes in living conditions and the possession of material goods. It is also important to realise what were the difficulties endured by our ancestors throughout their harsh lives.

# BEFORE 1700

There are few descriptions of the south-west from visitors before the 18th century. It would be exciting to have reports from Roman soldiers, Christian missionaries, Vikings, Norman barons, Cistercian monks and others, but unfortunately such accounts could now be only the work of writers of fiction. Regrettably any surviving accounts are usually brief and provide little information. Another drawback is that scarcely any accounts are available until the 17th century, partly reflecting the more peaceful conditions after the Union of the Crowns in 1603.

If people from modern times were whisked back to the south-west in the 17th century or earlier times, probably they would notice first of all the absence of cars, lorries and trains, the much lower population, and the poor housing and living conditions. Very conspicuous also would be mud-tracks instead of roads, the open unenclosed fields, the undrained bogs in the valleys, the absence of large forestry plantations and the small size of towns and villages. They would miss electric power, piped water, modern sanitation, television, telephones and computers. Going further back in time to the Middle Ages the visitor would see the huge, intact abbeys of the Cistercian monks. Nearby they would see the busy activities of monks, lay-brothers and many other people. They would wonder how such a poor society could produce such architectural grace and perfection. Towering above the small huts of the peasants would be not only abbeys, but also great castles built of stone such as Threave, Caerlaverock and Cardoness. Earlier in time there would be timber motte-and-bailey castles, and preceding those the hill-forts with vitrified ramparts, such as the Mote of Mark. Life was perpetually insecure: food supplies depended on the weather and the absence of marauders; modern medicine, anaesthetics and surgery were not available. Superstitions and witchcraft were rife. On the other hand there were not the pressures of modern life, and the dangers of environmental pollution had not arisen.

The south-west was to some extent separated from the economy in the rest of the southern half of Scotland. Until the growth of Glasgow and the Atlantic trade in the 18th century the commercial centre of Scotland was the east coast with ships crossing the North Sea to continental countries. The south-west remained somewhat isolated from the main Scottish trading routes. It must be pointed out that Galloway looks across to Cumbria, the Isle of Man and Ireland. The accounts prior to 1700 show that Dumfries, Kirkcudbright, Stranraer and Portpatrick were already important in the economy of the south-west. Shifting sands and tidal problems, however, restricted the development of harbours along the Solway Firth.

Travel in Scotland was slow, difficult and at times dangerous before the development of a network of railway lines in the mid 19th century. Unless a journey could be made along the coast, most people had to walk or ride on horseback or travel in a cart. A particularly hazardous journey (see the accounts of John Taylor, Richard Franck and Celia Fiennes) was entering Scotland by fording the Rivers Esk and Sark, or at low tide the extensive sands near the mouth of the Esk. There is no River Solway. The name Solway was originally Sulwath meaning the muddy ford - probably at the mouth of the Esk.

# JOHN HARDYNG

Hardyng who lived from 1378 to about 1465 was born in the north of England. He served in the campaign of Agincourt in 1415 and in the sea-fight off Harfleur at the mouth of the Seine in 1416. He subsequently became involved in trying to obtain documents which would justify England's claims of suzerainty over Scotland. Hardyng concocted six documents allegedly found in Scotland. In the 19th century these were proved to be forgeries. In his later life he was for many years Constable of Kyme Castle in Lincolnshire.

His Chronicle contains an account of his visit to Scotland during the reign (1413-22) of Henry V who sent him there to seek supporting documents. The brief account of his visit in an otherwise lengthy Chronicle is primarily a report on how an English army could invade Scotland and obtain supplies from either the local countryside or a supporting English fleet. It highlights the perpetual threat from England which loomed over Scotland in the Middle Ages.

Hardyng rewrote the Chronicle several times to make it more appropriate for new patrons. It was written in verse. The following two stanzas refer to Galloway and Dumfries:

*From the town of Ayr in Kyle (1) to Galloway,*
*Through Carrick pass into Nithsdale,*
*Where Dumfries is a pretty town always,*
*And plentiful also of all good victuals*
*For all your army, without any fail.*
*So that keeping this journey, by my instruction,*
*That realm you shall bring in subjection.*

*Then from Dumfries to Carlisle you shall ride*
*23 miles of very ready way (2).*
*So may you win the land on every side*
*Within a year, without more delay.*
*For castles there is none that withstand you may,*
*Nor abide your siege against your ordinance(3)*
*So simple and weak is their purveyance (4).*

It is interesting to note his comment that there were good victuals [food] available in the Dumfries area. His omission of any reference to Caerlaverock Castle seems to confirm that in the early 15th century its defences were still awaiting repair.

**NOTES**

1. Ayrshire, running from north to south, is traditionally divided into Cunninghame, Kyle and Carrick.

2. A considerable underestimate of the distance.

3. Ordnance, artillery.

4. Purveyance refers to the provisioning of food.

# THE ENGLISH OFFICER'S REPORT

An unknown Englishman wrote a report on the feasibility of attacking Galloway, the western Borders and Ayrshire about 1563-66. The precise date is not known but references to the names of some landowners in the report narrow the date to those years. His report concentrated on suitable places for a landing by sea and the strength of the local castles. The background was that in those years Scotland was ruled by Mary, a Catholic, while Elizabeth, a Protestant, ruled England. Although the Church in Scotland by that time had become Protestant, there was the distinct possibility that Mary - perhaps with backing from France or Spain - would try to restore the Catholic Church in Scotland. That in turn would create dangers for Elizabeth.

The original document is in the British Library (1). Unfortunately some pages at the beginning - probably covering Wigtownshire - are missing, and the document was also damaged in a fire in the Cottonian Library in 1731. The surviving pages (2) include four drawings: a sketch of a castle which is probably Cruggleton, a plan of Kirkcudbright bay and town, a sketch of Caerlaverock Castle and a plan of Annan. If the first sketch does show Cruggleton, that is particularly interesting and important as Cruggleton (which was once a major stronghold) was demolished in the course of the 17th century (3). The plan of Kirkcudbright shows the High Street and also the Priory to the south of the town on the eastern side of St. Mary's Isle. The Priory subsequently became the house associated with the Earl of Selkirk and John Paul Jones. A monk's well is still shown nearby on modern maps. Another significant point is that the plan shows no sign of the castle which had been built in the late 13th century at what is now called Castledykes. This important castle must have been dismantled between 1508 (when James IV stayed there) and the early 1560's. It would be unwise to assume too much accuracy in the details of these drawings, and they should probably be regarded to a large extent as representational.

The report contains information pertaining mainly to possible military and naval enterprises, but there are interesting comments on other matters. He reported that Wigtown was a *strait (difficult) haven to come in at, by reason of narrow sands, contrarious streams and shallows.* He commented on the difficulty of capturing Cardoness Castle by either land or sea. Kirkcudbright was *the best port of all; ships at the ground ebb may arrive and lie within the isle of Ross, foranemptes [opposite] St. Mary's Isle; and at the full sea they may pass up and lie at all times under the freres*

From:- *"Military Report on the West March and Liddesdale… by an English Official between the years 1563 and 1566."*

*[friary] of the town. Further east there may come ships to the Carsethorn, under the hill called Sernfell (Criffel), and no farther, being open riding without any haven, and dangerous for sundry winds. Distant from Dumfries 8 miles, to which boats of 10 tons may arrive.* Nithsdale, he reported, was *a country plenteous of corn and beasts.* The people of Annandale were *all light horsemen, very expert in that, especially within their own country, being a straight ground and well knowledged thereof.*

**NOTES**

1. The reference is Cotton Ms.Titus.C.XII and it is described as *A topographical and military account of the state of the marches, with illuminated drawings of some castles.*

2. Part of the text of the report and also enlarged colour reproductions of the four drawings are included in "The History of Lidddesdale, Eskdale, Ewesdale, Wauchopedale and the Debateable Land by R.B.Armstrong," Part I, (1888).

3. For further details see G.Ewart's 'Cruggleton Castle. Report on Excavations 1978-81' (1985).

# JOHN TAYLOR

John Taylor (1580-1653) was born in Gloucestershire. He served in the English fleet against the Spanish and subsequently became a Thames water-man. Although he had no real ability as a poet, he could put together rhymes and he gave himself the title of 'the king's water-poet and the queen's water-man'. He had a ready wit and a taste for eccentric behaviour. Taylor enjoyed travelling within Britain and also on the continent, and he visited Scotland in the late summer and early autumn of 1618. He subsequently wrote and published an account of his travels. This was partly poetry and partly prose. A sub-title to his 'Penniless Pilgrimage' stated that it would explain: *How he travelled on foot from London to Edinburgh, not carrying any money to or fro, neither begging, borrowing or asking meat, drinking or lodging.*

> *'Eight miles from Carlisle runs a little river, (1)*
> *Which England's bounds, from Scotland's grounds does sever.*
> *Without horse, bridge or boat, I o'er did get*
> *On foot, I went, yet scarce my shoes did wet.*
> *I being come to this long-looked-for land,*
> *Did mark, remark, note, renote, viewed and scanned;*
> *And I saw nothing that could change my will,*
> *But that I thought myself in England still.*
> *The kingdoms are so nearly joined and fixed,*
> *There scarcely went a pair of shears betwixt;*
> *There I saw sky above, and earth below,*
> *And as in England, there the sun did show'.*

Taylor's first impressions of Scotland were more favourable than those of some other visitors. Subsequently he went north to Moffat.

*My first night's lodging in Scotland was at a place called Moffat, which, they say is thirty miles from Carlisle, but I suppose them to be no longer than forty of such miles as are between London and St. Alban's (but indeed the Scots do allow almost as large measure of their miles as they do of their drink, for an English gallon, either of ale or wine, is but their quart, and one Scottish mile, now and then, may well stand for a mile and a half or two English) (2); but howsoever short or long, I found that day's journey the weariest that I had ever footed; and at night being come to the town I found good ordinary country entertainment; my fare and my lodging was sweet and good, and might have served a far better man than myself, although myself have had many times better: but this is to be noted, that though it rained not all the day, yet it was my fortune to be well wet twice, for I waded more than four miles distance from Carlisle in England, and at night, within two miles of my lodging I was fain (3) to wade over the river of Annan in Scotland, from which river the county of Annandale has its name.*

Taylor then travelled through Peeblesshire to Edinburgh, Stirling, Perth and Elgin before returning south to England. He seems to have depended on the courtesy and hospitality of the Scots for his maintenance. In his epilogue he claimed:

> *Thus did I neither spend, or beg, or ask,*
> *By any course, direct or undirectly.*

**NOTES**

1. The river Sark.

2. The old long Scots mile was 1984 yards. In 1855 the mile for the British Empire was standardised at 1760 imperial standard yards. It is likely that in earlier times there was a wide range of interpretations of a mile in Scotland. Taylor travelled probably about 40 modern miles to Moffat.

3. Fain would probably mean 'willing under the circumstances'.

# WILLIAM LITHGOW

Lithgow, the son of a merchant, was born in Lanark about 1582 and was educated there. About 1607 he set out to visit, mainly on foot, several countries in Europe. In 1609 he travelled from Paris to Italy and Greece and then to the Eastern Mediterranean and Egypt before returning to London. Within a year he set out on a second peregrination visiting Geneva, Italy, Tunis, Morocco, the Sahara and then Eastern Europe. On a third peregrination he was arrested and tortured in Spain as an alleged spy. A full account of his 'Rare Adventures and Painful Peregrinations' was published in 1632. He also wrote several other books and poems. His nickname was 'Cut-lugged Willie' as his ears had been mutilated over a love affair before he set out on his travels. He died about 1645 in the parish of Lanark.

In 1627 he travelled to Scotland from London, visiting the Western Isles and arriving in Arran in 1628. From there he went to Galloway. The following extracts are taken from the 1632 edition of his book:

*The Mull of Galloway and the South Rhins, c1590 from Blaeu's Atlas of Scotland, 1654, based on Timothy Pont's survey.*

I coasted Galloway even to the Mull that butteth into the sea, with a large Promontory, being the south-most part of the Kingdom. And thence footing all that large country to Dumfries and so to Carlisle: I found here in Galloway in divers road-way inns, as good cheer, hospitality, and serviceable attendance as though I had been ingrafted in Lombardy or Naples.

The wool of which country is nothing inferior to that in Biscay of Spain; providing they had skill to fine, spin, weave and labour it as they should. Nay, the Calabrian (1) silk had never a better lustre and softer grip than I have seen and touched this growing wool there on sheep's backs; the mutton whereof excels in sweetness. So this country abounds in beasts, especially in little horses, for which mettle and riding, may rather be termed bastard barbs (2) than Galloway nags (3).

Likewise their nobility and gentry are as courteous and every way generously disposed, as either discretion would wish and honour command; that (Cunninghame (4) being excepted, which may be called the Academy of Religion for a sanctified clergy and a godly people) certainly Galloway  is become more civil of late than any maritime country bordering with the western sea.

**NOTES**

1. Calabria is in the south of Italy.

2. Horses of a breed native to Barbary, a general designation at that time for the part of North Africa now comprising  Morocco, Algeria, Tunisia and Libya.

3. Galloway horses were small, hardy and well-suited to travelling on moors and  in hilly country. They were not suitable for the heavier work on farms, and after they were no longer required for military purposes they became scarce during the 18th century and extinct in the 19th century. Shakespeare in King Henry the Fourth Part Two, Act 2, Scene 4 referred to Galloway nags.

4. Cunninghame is the northern part of Ayrshire, which is traditionally divided into Cunninghame, Kyle and Carrick.

# SIR WILLIAM BRERETON

Sir William Brereton was a Cheshire gentleman who lived from 1604 to 1661. In 1634 and 1635 he travelled widely in the Low Countries and in Scotland and Ireland, and subsequently compiled a record of his Travels from his notes. He was a Puritan and a man of strong religious faith. At that time many of the Puritans were involved in developing settlements in North America away from the oppression of the religious policies of Charles I. Brereton's name appears in a list of those who held shares in 1630 in the Massachusetts Bay Company, but it is unlikely that he visited the colony. In 1640 he was elected to the House of Commons. During the English Civil War he commanded the Parliamentary forces in Cheshire and some neighbouring counties. Although he was derided by the Royalists, he was a man of knowledge and intellect.

On his visit to Scotland in 1635 he passed along the east coast to Edinburgh and then crossed to the west coast. From Glasgow he went south to Irvine and Ayr and through Carrick to Galloway.

On 2 July *we came into Galloway about six miles from the chapel (1), and therein observed one of the widest, broadest, plainest moors that I have seen; it is much moss, but now so dry, as it is good hanking (2). Coming off this moor, we observed an eminent stone, and tried it with our knives, and it did ring and sound like metal. About eight hour we came to this long desired chapel, the town is thence denominated and so called. This*

*Stranraer c1812.*

is situated upon a long loch (3), four miles long, wherein the sea ebbs and flows. Here we found good accommodation (only wanted wheat bread) in Hughe Boyde's house; ordinary 6d (4), good victuals, well-ordered, good wine and beer, lodging and horse meat. This house is seated four miles from the Port Patrick, whence it is to Carlingwark (5) 32 miles; best lodging there is Tho. Hutton; thence to Dumfries 28 miles; best lodging is John Harstein; thence to Carlisle 24. (6)

On 4 July *we went from hence (7) to the Port Patrick, which is foul winter way over the mossy moors, and there we found only one boat, though yesternight there were fifteen boats here* At Portpatrick they hired a boat of about ten tons to cross over to Ireland.

**NOTES**

1. Stranraer used to be known as The Chapel. At the time of Brereton's visit there were two villages separated by a burn. The village on the east side of the burn was known as The Chapel (from a chapel dedicated to St. John). The village on the west was called Stranraer, and that name was becoming inclusive of The Chapel. The site of the old chapel was near Stranraer Castle in the present centre of the town.

2. A hank is a length of coiled thread or yarn.

3. Loch Ryan

4. An ordinary was a set meal at a fixed price in an inn.

5. Carlingwark is now the town of Castle Douglas

6. Brereton did not go to Carlingwark or Dumfries, but the distances quoted to him for the journeys from Portpatrick to Carlingwark and from Dumfries to Carlisle were considerable under-estimates, while the distance from Carlingwark to Dumfries was an over-estimate unless taken along the coast.

7. Stranraer

# THOMAS TUCKER

In 1655 Thomas Tucker was sent to Scotland by Cromwell's government to help to arrange the customs and excise there during the Cromwellian occupation. As he was Registrar to the Commissioners for the Excise in England, he was a responsible official, and his report dated 20 November, 1656 on the harbours in Scotland is therefore valuable. He visited various ports along the east coast and on the Firth of Clyde and then came south from Ayr to the Glenfoot (perhaps Lendalfoot).

*From the Glenfoot there is no creek up the Loch (Loch Ryan), until one comes as far as Stranraer, otherwise called the Chapel, being a small market town the side of the Loch, which would prove a pretty harbour for shelter of vessels, in time of storm to put in there, which is certainly very seldom and rare, in respect there is not now nor ever was any trade to be heard of here.*

*'Next to Stranraer is Girvellen (Port Garvilland, 1½ miles south-west of Corsewall Point), a creek, whither boats come and go to and from Ireland, and next to those two is Portpatrick, a place much frequented by those who have any trade or affairs towards Ireland, because of its nearness to that country, and convenience of transporting horse, cattle, and other materials for planting thither, which is the sole trade of these parts: as there is no harbour so no vessel of any burden can possibly come in.*

*'Then next to these are Whithorn and Wigtown, to the latter of which comes sometimes a small boat from England, with salt or coals.*

*'Between these and Kirkcudbright there is no creek nor port, but one creek at the foot of the water of Fleet, not worthy of the naming. As for Kirkcudbright, it is a pretty and one of the best ports on this side of Scotland, where there are a few, and those very poor, merchants, or pedlars rather, trading for Ireland. Beyond this, there are the small creeks of Balcarry, the Water of Urr, and Southerness, whither some small boats come from England with salt and coals. And last of all Dumfries, a pretty mercat town, but of little trade, that they have being most part by land, either for Leith or Newcastle. The badness of coming into the river upon which it lies, hindering their commerce by sea, so as whatever they have come that way is commonly and usually landed at Kirkcudbright.*

# RICHARD FRANCK

Franck was born in Cambridge about 1624 and died in 1708. When the English Civil War broke out, he joined the Parliament's Army and probably obtained the rank of Captain. He took part in Cromwell's invasion of Scotland in the early 1650s. About 1656-57 he returned to Scotland and travelled through much of the country. He may have undertaken this journey to avoid the disturbances which seemed likely to arise in England between Cromwell and the more extreme Puritan factions. He wrote his Northern Memoirs about this visit in 1658 but it was not published until 1694. It seems that at some time after the Restoration he crossed to America and wrote a philosophical treatise there, but it is not known when he returned.

His Memoirs take the form of a dialogue between two people called Arnoldus (himself) and Theophilus. Modern readers may find his style pompous and stilted, but nevertheless his Memoirs contain some interesting descriptions. His book also contains a considerable amount of information on angling, rivalling Izaak Walton's The Compleat Angler which was originally published in 1653.

Arnoldus and Theophilus approached Scotland from Carlisle. When they came to the Solway they found *a good guide to pilot us over these sinking sands.* Their guide told them to *haud a plack*(1) while he fetched his salmon-spear. He explained to them how he hunted the salmon.(2)

They proceeded to Dumfries. Franck recorded it as *anciently a town girt about with a strong stone wall(3); but the late irruptions, or perhaps some state disagreement, has in a manner defaced that regular ornament, otherwise the cankerous teeth of time have gnawn out the impressions, as evidently appear by those ruinous heaps. Nor is the Arnotus (the river Nith) in all parts portable (navigable), notwithstanding her shores are so delightful.'*

*In the midst of the town is their market-place, and in the centre of that stands their tolbooth, round about which the rabble sit, that nauseate the very air with their tainted breath, so perfumed with onions, that to an Englishman it is almost infectious.(4)*

*'But the kirk (the ancient church of St. Michael) is comely, and situated southward(5)… Here also you may observe a large and spacious bridge, that directly leads into the country of Galloway.(6)*

*The town of Dumfries from the east - from a pencil drawing by John McCormick, based on an original supposedly dated 1593.*

From Dumfries they went to Sanquhar. Franck described it as standing *situated on a flat or level, surrounded, as you see, with excellent cornfields: but more remote it's besieged with mountains that are rich in leadmines.*(7) Franck also mentioned that Sanquhar had a brew-house, a market-place, a tolbooth and a kirk. Subsequently they went to Glasgow and then into the Highlands, returning by the east coast.

## NOTES

1. A plack was a small Scottish coin issued between about 1470 and 1603, and the word was also used to indicate a very small amount. The phrase used by the guide would mean 'hold on a little'.

2. There are references to this mode of fishing in chapter XXVI in 'Guy Mannering' and letter IV in 'Redgauntlet.'

3. There is a description of the old town wall in W. McDowall's History of Dumfries, 4th Edition (1986), page 139, but this should be read with caution as he quoted no sources for his description.

4. The present Mid-Steeple in the middle of the High Street in Dumfries was built early in the 18th century, replacing the tolbooth seen by Franck.

5. St. Michael's Church was rebuilt in 1744-45.

6. The ancient 'Devorgilla' bridge in Dumfries is a 15th century structure replacing an earlier bridge associated with Devorgilla. In 1273 she founded Sweetheart Abbey in memory of her husband John Balliol. She also founded Balliol College in Oxford.

7. A reference to the mines in the vicinity of Wanlockhead and Leadhills.

# JOHN RAY

Ray, the son of a blacksmith, was born in Essex, in 1628. He studied at Cambridge University and became a Major Fellow of Trinity College in 1651. He was also an eminent preacher and was known for preaching solid and useful Divinity. After the Restoration of Charles II he refused to subscribe to the religious Act of Uniformity (which imposed the Anglican forms of worship), and he gave up his Fellowship in 1662. Ray became a distinguished botanist and ornithologist and in 1667 was admitted as a Fellow of the Royal Society. He died in 1705. His itineraries were published in 1740.

In 1661 Ray travelled to Scotland visiting Dunbar, Edinburgh, Stirling and Glasgow. On his return south from Glasgow he rode through Hamilton and Douglas to Dumfries. Ray travelled widely elsewhere as far as Whitby, St. David's Head and Land's End and on the continent. He provided a lengthy account of his visit to Dumfries, describing especially religious observances.

*24 August - We rode to Dumfreis, or (as they spelled it) Drumfrese, twenty-eight miles, and in the way saw lead mines, at a place called the Lead Hills, which will in time, it is likely, increase to a good considerable town. We also passed over much hilly ground; the highest place was called Anderkin-Hill,(1) upon the top whereof the air was sharp and piercing, when in the level it was warm and gentle: neither yet were we on the highest apex of it, by the ascent of near half a mile, as we guessed. This hill we judged to be higher than any we had been upon in England or Wales, Snowdon itself not excepted(2). This is a dangerous passage in winter time, the way being narrow and slippery, and a great precipice on the one hand, besides the descent steep, so that we led our horses down about a mile.(3)*

*At Dumfries they have two ministers, one a young man named Campbell, related (as we were told) to the Marquis of Argyle, the other, an elder man, by name, Henderson, who has married his daughter to the younger. Campbell prayed for the preservation of their church government, and discipline, and spoke openly against prelacy and its adjuncts and consequences. Here, as also at Dunbar, and other places, we observed the manner of their burials, which is this: when any one dies, the sexton or bell-man goeth about the streets, with a small bell in his hand, which he tinkleth all along as he goeth, and now and then he makes a stand, and proclaims who is dead, and invites the people to come to the funeral at such an hour. The people and minister many times accompany the corpse to the grave at the time appointed, with the bell before them, where there is nothing said, but only the corpse laid in.*

*St. Michael's Church, Dumfries, from a pencil drawing by John McCormick,
based on a 17th century original.*

*The minister there, in the public worship, does not shift places out of the desk into the pulpit, as in England, but at his first coming in, ascends the pulpit. They commonly begin their worship with a psalm before the minister comes in, who, after the psalm is finished, prayeth, and then reads, and expounds in some places, in some not; then another psalm is sung, and after that their minister prays again, and preacheth as in England.*

*Before sermon, commonly, the officers of the town stand at the church-yard gate, with a join'd stool and a dish, to gather the alms of all that come to church. The people here frequent their churches much better than in England, and have their ministers in more esteem and veneration. They seem to perform their devotions with much alacrity. There are few or no sectaries or opinionists(4) among them; they are much addicted to their church government, excepting the gentry, who love liberty, and care not to be so strictly tied down(5).*

*26 August - We bade farewell to Scotland, and after a journey of twenty-four miles, arrived at Carlisle, fording three rivers by the way, one at Annan, which, by reason of our ignorance, might have been a dangerous pass to us(6).*

**NOTES**

1. Anderkin is Enterkin.

2. This shows the lack of precision at that time over the heights of mountains. Snowdon is 1,085 metres. The highest of the Lowther Hills near Leadhills is only 732 metres.

3. See also the accounts of John Macky and Daniel Defoe early in the following century on the hazards of the Enterkin Pass.

4. As an English nonconformist, Ray presumably used the terms sectaries or opinionists in their English context. They were not in Scottish usage. Various sects in the English Puritan movement, such as the Independents and the Baptists, dissented from the Church of England on several grounds.

5. The gentry tended to favour the Episcopalian system as they resented the discipline of the kirk-sessions in the Presbyterian system. After the Restoration of Charles II in 1660 bishops were superimposed again on the Presbyterian framework, and the General Assembly was no longer summoned. 262 ministers, mainly from Glasgow southwards to Ayrshire, Galloway and Dumfriesshire, refused to comply and were ejected from their churches.

6. One of the greatest hazards in travelling was fording rivers due to the lack of bridges.

# JAMES BROME

James Brome, who was a clergyman of the Church of England, visited Scotland in 1669. He travelled along the east coast to Edinburgh, crossed over to Glasgow, and like John Ray went south by Hamilton towards Dumfries. He and his companions had a difficult journey for two days over wide moors and dangerous mountains and through a countryside where food was scarce. In 1700 he published his account of his journeys under the title of Travels over England, Scotland and Wales. In 1712 he published another book of his travels covering Portugal, Spain and Italy. He died in 1719.

*But coming at length to Dumfries in the County of Nithsdale it made us some amends, for being situated between two hills upon the mouth of the river Nith, over which is laid a bridge of large fine stones, it appears to be one of the most flourishing towns in this*

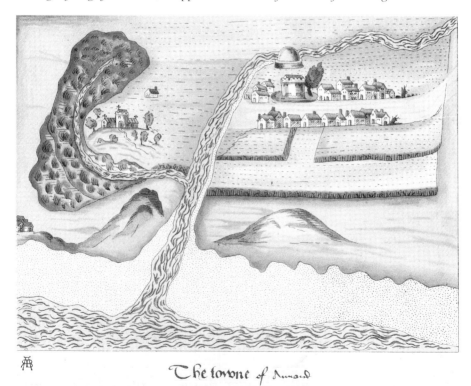

The town of Annan from:- "Military Report on the West March and Liddesdale… by an English Official between the years 1563 and 1566."

*tract, notable no less for its ancient castle and manufacture of cloth, than for the murder of John Comyn, one of the most renowned personages for his retinue and equipage in all this kingdom, whom Robert Bruce, for fear he should forestall his way to the crown, ran quite through with his sword in the Friars Church(1), and soon obtained his pardon from the Pope, though he had committed so great a murder in so sacred a place'.*

*'After this we came to Annan at the mouth of the river Annan in the County of Annandale, bordering upon our own nation, which lost all its glory and beauty upon the war, which was raised in Edward the Sixth's days(2); in these two last-named counties have been bred a sort of warlike men, who have been infamous for robbery and depredations, for they dwell upon Solway-Firth, a fordable arm of the sea at low water, through which frequently they have made many inroads into England to fetch home great booties, and in which they were wont after a delightful manner on horseback, with spears to hunt salmons, of which there are in these parts a very great abundance.*

**NOTES**

1.  Comyn was murdered in February 1306. Although Bruce's supporter, Bishop Wishart of Glasgow, soon absolved him from his sins, the Pope in May 1306 passed sentence of excommunication on Bruce for sacrilege. The Papacy released Bruce from excomunication in October 1328.

2.  Edward VI of England was born in 1537 and reigned from 1547 to 1553. During his reign the English continued to inflict on the Scots 'The Rough Wooing' started by his father, Henry VIII. The purpose of the repeated invasions was to force the Scots to agree to the marriage of Edward to the young Mary Queen of Scots. Dumfries was sacked and Dumfriesshire devastated.

# CELIA FIENNES

Celia Fiennes (1662-1741) was the unmarried grand-daughter of Viscount Saye and Sele, one of the leaders of the opposition to Charles I in England and nicknamed 'Old Subtlety.' The son of one of Celia's cousins was General 'Hangman' Hawley whose army was beaten by the Jacobites at Falkirk in 1746.

In her preface to her account of her journeys she explained that 'they were begun to regain my health by variety and change of aire and exercise'. She rode on horseback and was accompanied by a couple of servants. Between 1685 and 1703 she visited most parts of England from Land's End to Dover, East Anglia, Shrewsbury and Hadrian's Wall. Celia's book provides a comprehensive account of England at that time.

In 1698 after reaching Carlisle she took a guide and *so went for Scotland,* fording the Esk which she described as *very broad and hazardous to cross even when the tyde is out.* Unfortunately her visit to Scotland was very brief and she went only a few miles over the Border. Celia did not go further as she was uncertain of finding accommodation. As Celia was very observant her account of what she saw in 1698 is a valuable portrait of living conditions in the countryside at the end of the 17th century. Her Journal was first published in 1888.

*Thence I went into Scotland over the river Sark which is also flowed by the sea but in the summer time is not so deep, but can be passed over though pretty deep but narrow; it affords good fish but all here about which are called Borderers seem to be very poor people which I impute to their sloth; Scotland this part of it is a low marshy ground where they cut turf and peat for the fuel, though I should apprehend the sea might convey coals to them; I see little that they are employed besides fishing which makes provision plentiful, or else their cutting and carving turf and peat which the women and great girls bare legged does lead a horse which draws a sort of carriage the wheels like a dung-pot and hold about 4 wheel barrows; these people though with naked legs are yet wrapped up in plaids a piece of woollen like a blanket or else riding hoods, and this when they are in their houses; I took them for people which were sick seeing 2 or 3 great wenches as tall and big as any women sat hovering between their bed and chimney corner all idle doing nothing, or at least was not settled to any work, though it was nine of the clock when I came thither, having gone 7 long miles that morning.*

*This is a little Market town called Adison Bank(1) the houses look just like the booths* at a fair - I am sure I have been in some of them that were tolerable dwellings to these - they have no chimneys their smoke comes out all over the house and there are great holes in the sides of their houses which lets out the smoke when they have been well smoked in it; there is no room in their houses but is up to the thatch and in which are 2 or 3 beds even to their parlours and buttery; and notwithstanding the cleaning of their parlour for me I was not able to bear the room; the smell of the hay was a perfume and what I rather chose to stay and see my horses eat their provender in the stable than to stand in that room, for I could not bring myself to sit down; my landlady offered me a good dish of fish and brought me butter in a Lairdly Dish with the clap bread(2), but I could have no stomach to eat any of the food they should order, and finding they had no wheaten bread I told her I could not eat their clapt oat bread, so I bought the fish she got for me which was full cheap enough, nine pence for two pieces of salmon half a one near a yard long and a very large trout of an amber colour; so drinking without eating some of their wine, which was exceeding good claret which they stand conveniently for to have from France, and indeed it was the best and truest French wine I have drank this seven year and very clear, I had the first tapping of the little vessel and it was very fine.

Then I went up to their church which looks rather like some little house built of stone and brick such as our ordinary people in a village live in: the doors were open and the seats and pulpit was in so disregarded a manner that one would have thought there was no use of it, but there is a parson which lives just by whose house is the best in the place and they are all fine folks in their Sundays clothes; I observe the church-yard is full of grave stones pretty large with coats of arms and some had a coronet on the escutcheons(3) cut in the stone; I saw but one house that looked like a house about a quarter of a mile, which was some gentlemans, that was built 2 or 3 rooms and some over them of brick and stone the rest were all like barns or huts for cattle.

This is threescore miles from Edinburgh(4) and the nearest town to this place is 18 miles, and there would not have been much better entertainment or accommodation and their miles are so long in these countries made me afraid to venture, least after a tedious journey I should not be able to get a bed I could lie in.

**NOTES**

1. Probably the village of Allison Bank (now vanished), adjoining Gretna Green.

2. Lairdly is lordly or lavish. Clap bread is a thin oatmeal cake.

3. A shield having a coat-of-arms.

4. Edinburgh is about 80 modern miles from where she was.

# THE 18TH CENTURY

The precise state of living conditions is the south-west in the 1790's is known in far more detail than for any preceding era. This was due to the publication of the Statistical Account of Scotland at that time. This comprised accounts of each parish written usually by the parish minister and collated for each county.

There were remarkable changes in the course of the 18th century, especially in the closing decades. These changes were due at least partly to the eclipse of the Jacobites in 1746 and the ensuing political stability. After many centuries in which conditions had been almost static, there was a surge of progress. Dwellings were constructed in more durable materials; the risk of widespread famine receded with the introduction of a wider range of crops(1) and improved farming techniques; families accumulated more household goods; more attention was given to the condition of the roads(2); and the provision of schools improved. The appearance of the countryside began to change with the enclosure of fields. Population started to increase, and the numbers in the three counties grew from 77459 in 1755 to 106726 in 1801.

The late 18th century saw the development of several 'planned villages' in the south-west. These were created by landowners. Some towns which are now quite old and well-established were developed as planned villages, such as Port William, Garlieston, Gatehouse of Fleet, Dalbeattie and Castle Douglas. These developments have therefore to be kept in mind when reading earlier accounts.

It is surprising that the development of smuggling did not attract comments from visitors. Many coves along the Solway coast were used by smugglers for landing their wares, and there were tracks leading out of Galloway regularly used by the smugglers and their pack-horses. There is, however, a reference to smugglers in Lockhart's life of Scott. In the 1790s Scott regularly visited Liddesdale, accompanied by Robert Shortreed, Sheriff-Substitute of Roxburghshire. Shortreed's son informed Lockhart that one evening when the Bible was being read after supper, the pious exercise of the household was hopelessly interrupted by the clatter of horses' feet and the arrival of a keg of brandy from the Solway Firth(3).

The decay of some of the great mediaeval buildings continued during the 18th century. The growing use of stones for building houses and for enclosing fields with dykes led to the clearance of many stones not only from the fields but also from the old abbeys and deserted castles. They fell more and more into a state of dilapidation until in the late 18th century or subsequently some of them passed into the guardianship of owners or trustees who tried to preserve what was left of the ruins. Bishop Pococke's account has interesting descriptions of the ruins at Whithorn, Dundrennan and Sweetheart Abbey in 1760.

In comparison with the 17th century there were far more visitors going to Scotland in the 18th century. This increase stemmed from the increasing political security, improvements in the roads, and the growing romantic legend of the '45. Following Dr. Johnson's famous visit in 1773, it became fashionable for English people to make a tour in Scotland, but they usually headed for the Highlands and neglected to explore Dumfries and Galloway.

**NOTES**

1.  See John Wesley's Journal for 14 May, 1788.

2.  See John Wesley's Journal for 12 May, 1788, but note also his entry for 26 March, 1767 on crossing the Solway Firth. There was no bridge over the Esk until the early 19th century.

3.  See J. G. Lockhart's Memoirs of Sir Walter Scott, chapter VII (1792-1796).

# JOSEPH TAYLOR

Very little is known about Taylor except that he was a barrister of the Inner Temple in London who travelled with two friends in August 1705 from London via York to Edinburgh. He was far from complimentary about Scotland and the Scots. His visit took place at a time when there was considerable popular agitation over friction between the Scottish and English Parliaments. Taylor left Edinburgh on 8 September and returned south through Linton and Moffat to Carlisle. The following passages are from his book 'A Journey to Edenborough in Scotland.'

*… about 4 in the afternoon, we were obliged to proceed on our journey to Moffat, a market town, where we were informed we should meet with good lodging, which made us ride on the more briskly, but notwithstanding all our speed, we had such terrible stony ways, and tedious miles, that when we thought we had been near the place, we met a Scotchman, who told us we were not got half way. This put us almost into the spleen, for we could see nothing about us, but barren mountains on the right, and the River Tweed on the left, which running through the stones and rocks with a terrible noise seemed to us like the croaking of a Raven, or the tone of a Screech Owl to a dying man, so we were forced to ride on by guess, knowing not a step of the way, and meeting none to direct us, till at last coming up a hill, we spied some wagons going over another mountain before us, and resolving to press somebody into our service, we rode on as fast as we could to overtake them. 'Twas now duskish, and we found the wagons laden with wine to be transported privately into England. The man that looked after the wagoners, seeming to be a servant, we seized upon him, and with much persuasion, and the temptation of half a dollar(1), a sum large enough to bribe a Scot, we prevailed with him to leave his trust, like an honest man, and go with us, he told us we had still 12 long miles to Moffat. We followed our guide through dismal ways, over the ridges of dangerous precipices, till at last we came to a prodigious mountain called Eric Stane Hill, from a stone there set up by one Eric. Here we were obliged to alight, the ways being so stony that we had much ado to walk. When we were upon the top, the fellow told us of an English gentleman, who having lately lost his way, with his tutor and servant, was here obliged to take up his lodging on a bed of stones. After a great deal of fatigue, we got to the bottom with a world of joy (the fellow having likened to have lost his way) and he was so sensible of the danger in going back, that he told us he would give a shilling to be at home himself. This mountain has abundance of cross roads upon it, and is so very high, that in a clear day, one may see 40 miles into England, we now rode on with some hopes of arriving at our journey's end in a short time. About 2 miles off Moffat, we met a great company of Scotchmen with their cloaks and caps, which made us wonder at the reason of it, in so late an hour as 11*

at night, but upon enquiry found they had been at a funeral, (it being the Scotch custom for all the country to come in on such occasions) at last we arrived at Moffat.

This town is governed by a Provost, and is famous for its spa, which in summer time is frequented by most of the nobility of Scotland, therefore we expected it to be a place of good entertainment. Our Inn happened to be the provost's house, who being at the door, we took him for the ostler, and gave him our horses with a charge to take care of them, but we afterwards found them in the carthouse, with only a little oatstraw to feed upon, so that before we got out of Scotland they looked like skeletons. As for our own accommodation we called for the Tapster, and by and by, Mr. Provost came to us in that capacity, nay he did not disdain the office of a bootcatcher, so we took him for a jack of all trades. We here met with good wine and some mutton pretty well dressed, but looking into the beds, found there was no lying in them, so we kept on our clothes all night, and enjoyed ourselves by a good fire, making often protestations never to come into that country again.

September the 9th early in the morning, we sent for some of the spa water, which is much like that of Knaresborough(2), but not quite so strong, nor of so great virtue. After we had taken a view of the town, which seemed to be only a knot of hovels, we set forwards for Ecclefechan, and after a tedious journey, within 3 miles of the place, Mr. Harrison and I lost our way upon the moors, but Mr. Sloman being behind, met a Scotch Laird upon the road, who perceiving us to be strangers, told him he believed we were wrong, and so sent Harry to call us into the road again, but as the poor fellow was halloing to us, his horse leapt into a quagmire, where he had much ado to get him out.

Subsequently they went by Ecclefechan to Carlisle.

**NOTES**

1. The word dollar is a modified form of thaler, an ancient Germanic silver coin. The dollar in various forms of the name was used in the past in many European countries. In 1787 it became the standard coin in the U.S.A.

2. Knaresborough is in North Yorkshire near Harrogate.

# JOHN MACKY

John Macky was a Scotsman of good education but nothing is known about his parentage and birth. He became a government agent or spy in the early 1690s. In 1693 he was appointed inspector of the coast from Harwich to Dover in order to prevent treasonable correspondence between England and France. For some years he was involved in similar work. He died in 1726.

His book entitled 'Memoirs of his Secret Services during the reign of King William, Queen Anne and King George I' was published posthumously in 1733. He also wrote 'A Journey through England' (1714) and 'A Journey through Scotland' (1723). His description of his visit to Scotland is in the form of letters to a friend, but no dates are given on them.

Macky travelled from the Isle of Man to Kirkcudbright, which he described as *an ancient town with the prettiest navigable river I have seen in Britain.* The town consisted of *a tolerable street, the houses all built with stone, but not at all after the manner of England; even the manners, dress and countenance of the people, differ very much from the English. The common people wear all bonnets instead of hats, and though some of the townsmen have hats, they wear them only on Sundays, and extraordinary occasions. There is nothing of the gaiety of the English, but a sedate gravity in every face, without the stiffness of the Spaniards, and I take this to be owing to their praying and frequent long graces, which gives their looks a religious cast. Taciturnity and dullness gains the character of a discreet man, and a gentleman of wit is called a sharp man.*

*I arrived here on Saturday night, at a good inn; but the room where I lay, I believe, had not been washed in a hundred years. Next day I expected, as in England, a piece of good beef or a pudding to dinner; but my landlord told me, that they never dress dinner on a Sunday, so that I must either take up with bread and butter, a fresh egg, or fast till after the evening sermon, when they never fail a hot supper. Certainly no nation on earth observes the Sabbath with that strictness of devotion and resignation to the will of God. They all pray in their families before they go to church, and between sermons they fast; after sermon everybody retires to his own home, and reads some book of devotion till supper (which is generally very good on Sundays); after which they sing psalms till they go to bed.*

*The Macdweles, Mackys, Macquhys, Maclurgs, Maclellans and Maxwells, are the common names here(1), but gentlemen are never called by their names here, but, as in*

*France, by their estate. And indeed where so many gentlemen of the same name and surname live in the same county, it would make confusion in business if they were not distinguished by their designations. As for example, I know six gentlemen each called John Maxwell in this Stewartry. When you ask for any, you never name him, but his lairdship, as they call it. A lairdship is a tract of land with a mansion house upon it, where a gentleman has his residence, and the name of that house he is distinguished by. If you meet a man in the streets, and ask for Maxwell of Gribton(2), you ask for the Laird of Gribton, but if it is a knight, you mention both name and designation: Did you see Sir George Maxwell of Orchardton?*

*There is in the town a good old castle in tolerable good repair, with large gardens, which belonged to the family (Maclellans), but belongs now to the Maxwells.*

*Maclellan's Castle, Kirkcudbright, 1789 from "The Antiquities of Scotland" by Francis Grose, 1789-91.*

*There is fine salmon fishing in this river, and no place can be finer situated for a white-fish fishing on the Bank of Solway and the North Coast of Ireland, but the inhabitants neglect both, there being never a ship, and scarcely any boat belonging to the whole town. But the Union having encouraged both English and Scots to improve the fishing on the coasts and in the rivers of Scotland, it's to be hoped that this well situated town for that trade may in time come to flourish.*

From Kirkcudbright he went to Dumfries *along the best road I ever knew, being spacious and hard under foot… There is neither hedge nor ditch by the road's side, as in England, but wherever you see a body of trees, there is certainly a laird's house, most of them old towers of stone, built strong, to prevent a surprise from inroads, which were frequent between the two nations before the Kings of Scotland came to the Crown of England.*

On the way to Dumfries he visited Dundrennan Abbey, New Abbey and Terregles. *I passed the River Nith from Galloway to Dumfries over a fair stone bridge of thirteen large arches, the finest I saw in Britain next to London and Rochester. There is a street that leads from the bridge by an easy ascent to the castle(3), which is on the east side of the town, and has a commanding prospect of the town and adjacent country. This castle belonged also to the Earl of Nithsdale, and from it the High Street runs by an easy descent to the Church at half a mile's distance.*

*The High Street is spacious, with good stone buildings on each side; those on the north side having their hanging gardens to the river side.*

*The exchange and town-house are about the middle of the street towards the south, and besides this great street, Lochmaben - street has very good houses. This is a very thriving town, and has a good face of trade, yet their shipping don't come up within two miles of the town. The country round this town is very pleasant, and strewed with gentlemen's seats, all finely planted with trees, the great ornament of seats here.*

After Dumfries he made a little excursion into Annandale and then proceeded up the banks of the Nith *through a most beautiful country* to Drumlanrig, where he admired the Palace. From Drumlanrig *I ascended a famous pass cut out on the side of a rock called Entrokin Path. This Path or Pass is near a mile to the top; and is very steep. There cannot above two go abreast, and the precipice is much more dreadful than Penmanmawr in Wales.* From the Leadhills he passed into Tweeddale and thence to the east coast. He visited Edinburgh, St. Andrews, Dundee, Aberdeen, Inverness (where they spoke as good English as at London) and then south-east, crossing Cairn o' Mount towards Tayside and to Lochleven, Stirling, Linlithgow and Edinburgh (where he was disappointed at not being allowed to see the Honours of Scotland). He then went to Hamilton, Glasgow, Dumbarton, Greenock and through Ayrshire to Loch Ryan. From Portpatrick he went to the ancient monastery of Whithorn and to Wigtown which he described as *a pretty good sea-port town, but the harbour not near so good as Kirkcudbright. Thence to the 'handsome seat, called the Caily, belonging to Alexander Murray of Broughton, with a large park, which feeds one thousand bullocks, that he sends once every year to the markets of England.(4)… opposite to this, on the other side of the River Fleet, stands a handsome seat, called Cardoness, belonging to Lieutenant Colonel Maxwell, with Parks and Enclosures also for feeding of cattle.* Macky made no further comments on his return journey.

## NOTES

1.  See Patrick Dudgeon's pamphlet 'Macs in Galloway' (1888). There is a copy in the National Library of Scotland.

2.  Gribton is north-west of Dumfries, south-west of Holywood, just over 1½ miles west of the A76, and between the dismantled railway line and the Cluden Water. Perhaps, however, Macky meant Gribtae, about 3 miles east of Kirkcudbright.

3.  The site of the mediaeval castle was to the south of the town in the area now called Castledykes. It was demolished by the English in the 14th century and replaced by a massive tower-caste called the New Wark in the vicinity of what is now Queensberry Square. In the 18th century about half of it was demolished due to its ruinous state, and there was further demolition in 1846. Macky's reference was to Maxwell's Castle. This was built in 1572 in the area of what is now Castle Street. By the early 18th century the castle had become ruinous. In 1723 the site was purchased to erect a second church as St Michael's Church could not accommodate all the worshippers. Work was begun in 1724 and it was opened in 1727 as the New Church or Kirk. It contained many stones from the castle. In 1866 it was taken down and replaced by Greyfriars Church, which was completed in 1868.

4.  The Murrays of Broughton had their original seat at Broughton, south-east of Sorbie in Wigtownshire. In 1740 Alexander Murray bought Broughton House in Kirkcudbright from Thomas Mirrie, who had built it in the 1730s. The House is now a museum associated with the artist E. A. Hornel. The Murray family subsequently built the impressive Cally House at Gatehouse of Fleet (now the Cally Palace Hotel). This family was not connected to Murray of Broughton, Prince Charles' Secretary in the '45, who subsequently gave evidence against some Jacobites.

# DANIEL DEFOE

*Daniel Defoe*

Defoe (1660-1731) is best known in modern times as the author of Robinson Crusoe. In addition to being a journalist and a novelist he was a political agent on behalf of the Whig ministers in London. He visited Scotland both before and after the Union of 1707 on government service. Between 1724 and 1726 Defoe published the three volumes of A Tour through the whole island of Great Britain. A substantial part of the third volume contained descriptions of his visits to Scotland. Although there are references to the Jacobite Rebellion in 1715, it is probable that his accounts are based on his visits at the time of the Union with some skilful updating and editing. Defoe gave quite a detailed description of the South of Scotland and the coastal belt on the east coast up to Aberdeen, across to Inverness and north to Duncansby Head but his account of Scotland beyond the Highland line is slight and vague. Defoe's accounts are in the form of long letters or chapters which are undated and not addressed. These describe tours in particular parts of Britain, such as South-western Scotland. Defoe probably put together information from various visits in compiling the descriptions of these itineraries.

*The first place of note we came to in Scotland was Annan, or as some call it, Annandale, as they do the county, though, I think, improperly. It was a town of note, and a sea-port, and having a good river and harbour, was esteemed a town of good trade, but it was not situated for strength and the English took it so often, and specially the last time burnt it to the ground, in that war so fatal to the Scots, in the reign of Edward VI that it never recovered. Here was a good salmon fishery, and a trade to the Isle of Man, and by that to Ireland. But as the face of trade is altered since that time, and by the ruins of the place the merchants, and men of substance, removed to Dumfries, the town continues, to all appearance, in a state of irrevocable decay…*

*From hence, keeping the sea as close as we could on our left, we went on due west to Dumfries, a sea-port town at the mouth of the River Nid, or Nith. Here, indeed, as in some other ports on this side the island, the benefits of commerce, obtained to Scotland by the Union, appear visible, and that much more than on the east side, where they seem to be little, if anything mended, I mean in their trade.*

*Dumfries was always a good town, and full of merchants. By merchants, here I mean, in the sense that word is taken and understood in England (viz.) not mercers and drapers, shopkeepers, etc. but merchant-adventurers, who trade to foreign parts, and employ a considerable number of ships. But if this was so before, it is much more so now, and as they have (with success) embarked in trade, as well as to England and to the English plantations, they apparently increase both in shipping and people, for as it almost every where appears, where trade increases, people must and will increase, that is, they flock to the place by the necessary consequences of the trade, and, in return, where the people increase, the trade will increase, because the necessary consumption of provisions, cloths, furniture, etc. necessarily increases, and with them the trade.*

*There is a very fine stone bridge here over the River Nith, as also a castle, though of old work, yet still good and strong enough, also an exchange for the merchants, and a Tolbooth, or town-hall for the use of the magistrates. They had formerly a woollen manufacture here. But as the Union has, in some manner, suppressed those things in Scotland, the English supplying them fully, both better and cheaper; so they have more than an equivalent by an open trade to all the English plantations, and to England itself.*

*The castle in this town, as well as that at Caerlaverock, near the mouth of the river, and opening to the Firth of Solway, was formerly belonging to the ancient family of Nithsdale. That last mentioned castle has been a very magnificent structure, though now, like its owner, in a state of ruin and decay.*

*We could not pass Dumfries without going out of the way upwards of a day, to see the castle of Drumlanrig, the fine palace of the Duke of Queensberry, which stands at twelve miles distance, upon the same river, the vale on either side of the river is pleasant, and tolerably good. But when these rapid rivers overflow their banks, they do not, like Nile, or even like the Thames, and other southern streams, fatten and enrich the soil, on the contrary, they lodge so much sand and splinters of stone upon the surface of the earth, and among the roots of the grass, that spoils and beggars the soils, and the water is hurried on with such force also, as that in a good light soil it washes the best part of the earth away with it, leaving the sand and stones behind it…*

*"The very fine stone bridge…" of Dumfries by Robert Riddell, c. 1780.*

[Drumlanrig] 'tis environed with mountains, and that of the wildest and most hideous aspect in all the south of Scotland, as particularly that of Enterkin, the frightfullest pass, and most dangerous that I met with, between that and Penmenmuir in North Wales.

Here [presumably near Drumlanrig-Ed.] we were surprised with a sight, which is not now so frequent in Scotland as it has been formerly, I mean one of their field meetings, where one Mr. John Hepburn, an old Cameronian(1), preached to an auditory of near 7,000 people, all sitting in rows on the steep side of a green hill, and the preacher in a little pulpit made under a tent at the foot of the hill; he held his auditory, with not above an intermission of half an hour, almost seven hours and many of the poor people had come fifteen or sixteen miles to hear him, and had all the way to go home again on foot…

From Drumlanrig I took a turn to see the famous pass of Enterkin, or Introkin Hill, It is, indeed, not easy to describe, but by telling you that it ascends through a winding bottom for near half a mile, and a stranger sees nothing terrible, but vast high mountains on either hand, though all green, and with sheep feeding on them to the very top; when, on a sudden, turning short to the left, and crossing a rill of water in the bottom, you mount the side of one of those hills, while, as you go on, the bottom in which that water runs down from between the hills, keeping its level on your right, begins to look very deep, till at length it is a precipice horrible and terrifying; on the left the hill rises almost perpendicular, like a wall, till being come about half way, you have a steep, unpassable

*Caerlaverock Castle, 1790, from "The Antiquities of Scotland" by Francis Grose, 1789-91*

*height on the left, and a monstrous cwm [Ed.] or ditch on your right, deep, almost as the monument is high, and the path, or way, just broad enough for you to lead your horse on it, and, if his foot slips, you have nothing to do but let go the bridle, lest he pulls you with him…*

*The first town on the coast, of any note, is Kirkcudbright, or as vulgarly called, Kirkubry. It must be acknowledged this very place is a surprise to a stranger, and especially one whose business is observation, as mine was.*

*Here is a pleasant situation, and yet nothing pleasant to be seen. Here is a harbour without ships, a port without trade, a fishery without nets, a people without business, and, that which is worse than all, they do not seem to desire business, much less do they understand it. I believe they are very good Christians at Kirkubry, for they are in the very letter of it, they obey the text, and are contented with such things as they have. They have all the materials for trade, but no genius to it, all the opportunities for trade, but no inclination to it. In a word, they have no notion of being rich and populous, and thriving by commerce. They have a fine river, navigable for the greatest ships to the town quay, a haven, deep as a well, sage as a mill-pond; 'tis a mere wet dock, for the little island of Ross lies in the very entrance, and keeps off the west and north west winds, and breaks the surge of the sea, so that when it is rough without, 'tis always smooth within. But, alas! there is not a vessel, that deserves the name of a ship, belongs to it, and, though here is an extraordinary salmon fishing, the salmon come and offer themselves, and go again,* and cannot obtain the privilege of being made useful to mankind, for they take very few of them. They have also white fish, but cure none, and herrings, but pickle none. In a word, it is to me the wonder of all the towns of North-Britain, especially, being so near England, that it has all the invitations to trade that nature can give them, but they take no notice of it. A man might say to them, that they have all the Indies at their door, and will not dip into the wealth of them, a gold mine at their door, and will not dig it…

The wester Galloway, which is also called the shire of Wigtown, from the town of Wigtown, its capital, runs out with a peninsula, so far into the sea, that from the utmost shores, you see the coast of Ireland very plain, as you see Calais from Dover, and here is the town of Port Patrick, which is the ordinary place for the ferry or passage to Belfast or other parts in Ireland. It has a tolerable good harbour, and a safe road, but there is very little use for it, for the packet boat, and a few fishing vessels are the sum of navigation…

The people of Galloway do not starve; though they do not fish, build ships, trade abroad, etc. yet they have other business, that is to say, they are mere cultivators of the earth, and in particular, breeders of cattle, such as sheep, the number of which I may say is infinite, that is to say, innumerable, and black cattle, of which they send to England, if fame lies not, 50 to 60,000 each year(2).

Besides the great number of sheep and runts(3), as we call them in England, which they breed here, they have the best breed of strong low horses in Britain, if not in Europe, which we call pads, and from whence we call all small truss - strong riding horses Galloways, These horses are remarkable for being good pacers, strong easy goers, hardy, gentle, well broke and above all, that they never tire, and they are very much bought up in England on that account.

By these three articles, the country of Galloway is far from being esteemed a poor country, for the wool, as well as the sheep, is a very great fund of yearly wealth to them, and the black cattle and horses are hardly to be valued.

But I was sick of Galloway, through which the travelling is very rough, as well for the road, as for the entertainment, except, that sometimes we were received by the gentlemen, who are particularly very courteous to strangers, merely as such, and we received many extra-ordinary civilities on that only account.

**NOTES**

1. The Cameronians were followers of the die-hard Covenanter, Richard Cameron, who was killed in 1680. During the '15 Rebellion Hepburn organised a force of about 320 Cameronians to resist the Jacobites.

2. This seems a considerable over-estimate. See A. R. B. Haldane, The Drove Roads of Scotland (1952), chapter 10.

3. A runt is a small cow.

# SIR JOHN CLERK OF PENICUIK

Clerk, who was born in 1684, was very talented and considered to be one of the most enlightened men of his age. He had a wide range of interests in Economics, Natural History and Antiquities including such topics as the effects of thunder on trees. His first wife was a daughter of the Earl of Galloway. From 1702 to 1707 he was the Member of Parliament for Whithorn.

On 27 August, 1721 he set out from Penicuik (south of Edinburgh) to visit his brother-in-law the Earl of Galloway at Glasserton near Whithorn. He travelled through the Enterkin Pass to Drumlanrig and then to Penpont, Tynron, Moniaive, Dalry and Minnigaff. The following descriptions are from his Journal(1): *Having never paid a visit to the Earl of Galloway and his family since February 1704 I resolved to go at this time and carry my eldest son with me to see his Mother's friends.*

*We took journey from Penicuik on the 27 of August 1721 in the afternoon and come to Dolphinton that night. Here we took up our night's quarters and my cousin the Laird was so good natured as to go along with us next morning.*

*On the 28 we dined at the Leadhills, had sorry accommodation either for ourselves or horses. We found the Earl of Hopetoun's mines going on as formerly and several smelting houses erected since I was here last.*

*Drumlanrig Castle, 1749 from a drawing by Paul Sandby.*

In the afternoon we left Wanlockhead on our right hand where the Duke of Queensberry has very good lead mines, and came to the pass at Enterkin. This is a straight descent for 400 or 500 yards and will be very difficult in winter, yet at this season the green hills and small rivulets descending from them made the place not altogether disagreeable. A little from this pass we came in sight of Drumlanrig, the seat of the Duke of Queensberry which, with the woody grounds about it, made a very fine prospect.

Drumlanrig is a very large house built by way of a square but the architecture looks very Gothic by reason of its round stairs and turrets. The house in the meantime affords no great conveniences for lodgers, being only a single house, one room entering through another, unless where a trance(2) is taken off the breadth of the floor to give secret passages as they found convenient. The principal stair is of timber and a mere bauble for its contrivance. There is a gallery here which runs along the front of the house, but it is too narrow for its length. Some pavilions and lead statues make up the principal ornaments of this place. The house is pretty well furnished with good prints and there are abundance of family pictures by Sir Godfrey Kneller and some other good hands.

The gardens are by far the finest in this kingdom. They are excellently laid out in the newest fashion with parterres(3), terraces, sloping banks, wildernesses, hedges, water works etc., and the Duke keeps daily at work a gardener and 26 men to dress them.

At night we lodged in a very good house about a quarter of a mile off, which the Duke built for a tilliesoul(4) as they are called. English people keep this house at the time and give very good entertainment.

In the morning of the 29 we continued our journey to the Old Clachan(5) where we came about twelve a clock. By the way we saw a pleasant enough country and passed by the Kirks of Penpont and Tynron, a little village called Moniaive belonging to Craigdarroch, as likeways we saw Craigdarroch's house, for instead of turning to our left at the last named village we went straight on and fell out of the road at this gentleman's house for a mile or two.

3 miles from the Old Clachan we came to a prodigious cairn of stones made of old by the Romans for a sepulchral monument as was their custom,(6) and next to it a small cairn begun by the Stuarts about 7 years ago by way of diversion. Here the road divides itself. That to the left leads to New Galloway and that to the right to the Old Clachan.

Having dined at the village we took horse again and passed the Water of Ken which was something swelled with rain that had fallen in the night. Below this ford is New

*Galloway, a Royal Burgh, and near to it the late Viscount of Kenmure's house. This house is now in the hands of the Commissioners of Enquiry for the public, being forfeited by the Viscount's rebellion in 1715. The country is here very straight but the house of Kenmure is finely situated on a rising ground in the midst of a fine wood and is watered by the foresaid water which forms a lake of about 3 or 400 yards in breadth and several miles in length. It abounds with fresh water fish of all sorts, for I had occasion to know something about it when I was last in this country. There are likewise abundance of water fowl upon it and several boats for the pleasure and convenience of the people who live near it. The Viscount had here a pleasure boat of his own making, for he was a great master in all sorts of handy crafts. He suffered death on Tower Hill in 1716 and his body lies buried at the little kirk near the Old Clachan where is the burial place of his family.*

*Kenmure Castle, 1789 from "The Antiquities of Scotland" by Francis Grose, 1789-91.*

From the Water of Ken we passed on through wild grounds and bad way till we came to the new bridge on the Water of Dee. This water afforded us some contemplations, for till of late it was frequently unpassable, and even when it was not in a flood the passage was very difficult by reason of many sharp rocks that lay in the ford. Near to this place we saw on our right hand the Moss of Raploch(7), memorable for a great battle fought between King Robert Bruce and the English(8). Bones, helmets, swords and daggers found here give evidence of it to this day, besides a constant tradition amongst the people.

*Our way after passing Ken grew worse and worse till we came to a hill called the Saddle Loup where the way lay along a steep rock. The mountains hereabouts are wild beyond imagination so that scarce anything in the Alps exceeds them. They afford very little pasturage except for goat and wild deer. However on any other occasion I could have been pleased with them, for they afforded plenty of game of all sorts, particularly Red Fowl and Heath Fowl.*

*After having passed with difficulty this ugly place we were saluted with 3 blasts of thunder that for their nearness astonished us and frightened our horses. These were followed next with such a deluge of rain that I do not remember to have ever seen the like.*

*We continued our journey through the mountains in great distress till we came to Minnigaff, a little village belonging mostly to the Laird of Dalgoner. On our right hand by the way about 2 miles from the village we saw the Garlies which is the ancient seat of the Stuarts of Galloway. It is situated in a wood and if it were not for the neighbourhood of the mountains it would prove a very advantageous habitation.*

*Galloway horses are bred in the moors of Minnigaff and about the rocky hills of Craignelder and Poultrybuie(9)… For a description of Galloway what follows shall suffice. This shire is more properly called the shire of Wigton, for Galloway comprehends in it the Stewartry of Kirkcudbright. It begins at the Water of Cree and takes in a large part of [a] peninsula of about 40 miles in circumference or more. The country is generally plain except towards the northmost parts of it. The soil is warm but thin and brings all sorts of garden fruits to greater perfection than any county of Scotland. The surface of the ground is full of small rocks and in many places covered with whins, broom, ferns etc. However, there is very good feeding for all sorts of cattle. Their grain is just bear(10) and oats black and white. Barley they have none, nor for ordinary any peas(11). Their culture of grains seems a little odd, for their bear sets as they call them are never changed. That ground which I saw carrying bear has produced nothing else in the memory of man. There are very little improvements here in planting, for their industry runs only on enclosures for black cattle which indeed brings them in from England a great deal of profit. Their dykes are of stone without mortar, very thinly built together. However they are such as answer sufficiently the end. I was persuading them to change their method by making their enclosures less and banking up quick set hedges for warming their grounds and keeping their cattle from storms which are frequent from the west seas. They alleged against this that the thinness of their ground would not allow them to make hedges, but this seemed of a piece with their obstinate persistence in the culture of their grains.*

*By these enclosures such as they are I had occasion to compute that they brought in ten thousand guineas to their country, for the price of their cattle is commonly paid in gold. Sometimes they drive them up to the English fairs and sometimes they sell them at home to Englishmen who come down and pay them ready money for what they carry off. By the bye, all this is not above a tenth of what Scotland gains from England at this time upon black cattle, for I have good reason to believe there is above £100,000 sterling yearly paid us on that score. The inhabitants of Galloway are much lessened since the custom of enclosing their grounds took place, for there are certainly above 20,000 acres laid waste on that account. The principal rivers of this shire are Cree and Bladnoch which produce abundance of salmon and trout. The sea here is very fertile in fish but the people are very lazy. Wigtown is the principal town of the shire but is not much better than Whithorn. However it stands on a very agreeable promontory near the sea and if it were in the hands of industrious men it would be much better than it is. Here is a sort of harbour for ships but the passage by reason of sandbanks is very dangerous so that, like Whithorn, drinking is the principal branch of trade.*

*Upon Monday the 7th I left Glasserton and came to Sorbie. My Lord would convey us this length and afterwards would not part with us till he had passed the Water of Bladnoch. The Brigadier, his brother, went on with us to the Clary(12) where he dined with my Lord Garlies and continued with him that night.*

*Next morning about 6 we took horse and passed the Water of Cree at the ford of Machermore (13) where we took our leave of Lord Garlies who would convey us to the other side in our way to Bargaly(14). Machermore is a very pleasant little seat belonging to a gentleman of a small fortune. From this place we came through a moor enclosed in most places to Bargaly. Here I saw a little convenient house upon the banks of a small rivulet, which wanted no embellishments that any house in Britain has, save only those things were not so nicely done. Here are gardens, orchards, parterres, orangeries, waterworks, fishponds, bagnios [hot houses], enclosures, arbors, wildernesses, woods, etc., with such a variety of fruit as I had not observed the like in any place of this country. He had grapes and figs of several sorts, 38 kinds of cherries, 40 of plums, near 80 kinds of apples and as many pears. He had likewise a fine collection of various sorts of shrubs and evergreens. This little paradise stands at the foot of the largest and wildest hill in Galloway(15) where there is scarcely any pasturage for goats, though I was told that in some places of it there are very large deer.*

*We returned backwards the same way we came and dined at the Old Clachan.* Thence to Drumlanrig, Durisdeer and Penicuik.

Clerk made several visits to the north of England. In 1731 he went to Penrith,

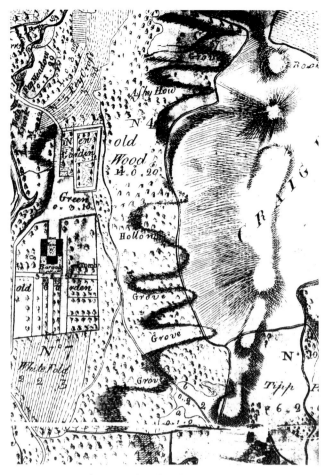

*Bargaly House and Gardens, from a survey of 1772.*

leaving Penicuik on 14 August and staying briefly at Drumcrieff, about 1½ miles south-east of Moffat on his way south(16). On Sunday the 15th he went to Moffat kirk. There was a collection for the poor who came to Moffat to drink the waters. On the next day he travelled to Ecclefechan. *The way all along was exceeding good. We had the Roman causeway for about 12 miles only for it turns off to the left over the hills about Lockerbie(17). There are several remains of Roman forts by the way(18). The causeway commonly runs in straight lines for a mile or half a mile with gravel above.* While he was at Ecclefechan he arranged to purchase three Roman stones from a temple in the fort at Birrens. On his return from England *we passed the firth very well, though there was some rain fallen but the tide was gone.* On his way north he collected the three stones.

Clerk went again to Galloway in 1735. The Earl's house at Glasserton had been burnt down, and the Earl wanted his advice on whether to rebuild it or plan a new house. He left Penicuik on 24 April. He stayed at Drumlanrig and then proceeded to Dalry and Minnigaff. The following descriptions are from his Memoirs of the journey(19).

*Minnigaff is a little country town situated on the Water of Cree. The tide flows near to it. On the other side is another country town called New Town Stuart. From thence to Clary, the seat of my Lord Garlies, eldest son to my Lord Galloway, is a fine road of 3 miles. Both sides are finely enclosed and belong to the Galloway family.*

*The Clary is a poor habitation but not small, for there is abundance of lodging about it but ill disposed and ruinous. On the south side of the gardens is the Moss of Cree, a vast slough of about 5 miles round and 20 foot deep of black moss, yet by draining several good improvements have been made out of it and many more will be made in time. Planting going well here but not in the moss where there is no earth. From the Clary I had a fine road of about 3 miles all along to Wigtown. This is a pleasant village situated on the sea side but has little or no trade. From Wigtown I rode along by Baldoon on my way to Whithorn. Baldoon is a very fine seat, having a navigable river on one side and the sea on the other. The enclosures are the finest in Galloway, lying for the most part on the seaside(20). The black cattle and sheep that are kept here bear the greatest price of any in Scotland. The first are of a middle kind finely shaped, the last carry wool equal to any sheep in England.*

On Sunday 11 May he went with the Earl and his wife to the kirk of Whithorn. *The steeple in old times served for a direction to sailors but it fell down lately and broke down some part of the church.*

On his return journey he was carried on a Customs House boat to Kirkcudbright. *This is a little town of very little trade but is pleasantly situated.* From Kirkcudbright he continued his journey on horse-back passing *a very pleasant lake with 2 islands covered with wood,* in or at a place called *Carlin's Werke*(21) and the Motte of Urr which he described as *an old religious mount*(22). After riding for 5 hours he reached Dumfries, and on 16 May returned to Penicuik in good health.

**NOTES**

1   The excerpts are from the article by W. A. J. Prevost in the Transactions of the Dumfries and Galloway Natural History and Antiquarian Society, vol. 41 (1962-63).

2   A passage.

3   A level space in a garden for flower beds.

4   This was usually accommodation for servants of guests if the host did not wish to entertain them at his own expense.

5   Dalry used to be called St. John's Clachan, as the church was dedicated to John the Baptist, patron saint of the Knights Templars who owned land there.

6   Presumably White Cairn near Corriedoo on the A702 about 4 miles east from Dalry. In the Statistical Account of Scotland (1791-99) it was described as 'a large pile of stones covered with a kind of whitish moss, which has therefore probably got the name of the White Cairn, and no doubt, like many others in Scotland, has been in ancient times a burial place.' The site has not been excavated, but the cairn is likely to be of early Bronze Age date. (Information from the Royal Commission on the Ancient and Historical Monuments of Scotland). The Account stated that the other cairn was said to be a monument to commemorate the killing of a wild boar by the first Knight of Lochinvar. The Stuarts mentioned by Clerk would not be the Royal House of Stuart but would probably be the Stewarts of Garlies on whom the title of Earl of Galloway had been conferred in 1623.

7   The Moss is now under the Clatteringshaws reservoir.

8   The tradition is that the King, aided by the sons of a widow alarmed the English in their camp on the Moss by gathering all the horses and goats in the neighbourhood so that the English during the night thought they were surrounded and did not leave the camp. The battle took place in the morning. See C. H. Dick's Highways and Byways in Galloway and Carrick, chapter XXXII and also Barbour's Bruce VII, line 237 onwards.

9   These hills are near Murray's Monument.

10  Bear (or Bere) was hardier but inferior in quality to the usual barley. Bere is pronounced bare and is now grown only in the north of Scotland.

11  Ordinary means a meal.

12  Mary Queen of Scots in her progress through Galloway in 1563 stayed at The Clary, at that time the Bishop's Palace. The building has disappeared but a local stream is called the Bishop Burn. (See 'Penninghame, the Story of a Parish' published in 1998).

13  This ford would have been between Carty and Newton Stewart.

14  Bargaly is on the Palnure Burn on the west side of Cairnsmore of Fleet.

15  Cairnsmore of Fleet is 711m. There are several higher mountains in Galloway including the Merrick 843m and Cairnsmore of Carsphairn 797m.

16  The following passages for 1731 are from 'Sir John Clerk's Journey to Penrith 1731' by W. A. J. Prevost and E. Birley in Transactions of the Dumfries and Galloway Natural History and Antiquarian Society, vol. XXXVII (1959-60).

17  Going towards the Roman fort at Birrens.

18  There was a Roman fortlet at Milton (Tassiesholm) about 3 miles south of Moffat.

19  The following passages for 1735 are from Sir John's 'Memoirs of a journie to Dumfrise shire and Galloway in 1735' in the article by W. A. J. Prevost in Transactions of the Dumfries and Galloway Natural History and Antiquarian Society, vol. XLII (1965).

20  The practice of enclosing fields for grazing was started in Wigtownshire by Sir David Dunbar of Baldoon in the last quarter of the 17th century. Enclosures led to the eviction of some of the smaller tenants in Galloway, and in 1724 there was a revolt by Levellers who overthrew dykes. The Revolt is part of the background to S. R. Crockett's novel 'The Dark o' the Moon'. Sir Walter Scott based the plot of 'The Bride of Lammermoor' on Dunbar's tragic first marriage.

21  In 1789 William Douglas, a prosperous merchant, bought the village of Carlingwark and soon transformed it into a planned village called Castle Douglas.

22  The Motte of Urr was a 12th century motte-and-bailey type of castle. The buildings have vanished, but the great earthwork is still a very impressive sight.

*Motte of Urr, from Grose's "Antiquities of Scotland", 1789.*

# JOHN WESLEY

*John Wesley*

John Wesley (1703-91), the famous preacher and founder of the Methodist Church, was a frequent visitor to Scotland. The entries in his Journal about Scotland are much kinder and more appreciative than those of some English travellers. Perhaps this was a reflection of his religion and the great happiness which he found in it and imported to others.

Wesley travelled frequently throughout the British Isles during much of his life. He visited Scotland 22 times between 1751 and 1790. Sometimes he entered Scotland going past Carlisle and other times along the east coast. He visited Dumfries nine times and several times crossed between Galloway and Ireland. On his visits he usually went to Glasgow and Edinburgh and sometimes further north to Dundee, Aberdeen and Inverness.

15 April 1753: *We dined at Dumfries, a clean, well-built town, having two of the most elegant churches (one at each end of the town) that I have seen. We reached Thorny-Hill in the evening. What miserable accounts pass current in England of the inns in Scotland. Yet here, as well as wherever we called in our whole journey, we had not only every thing we wanted, but every thing, readily, and in good order, and as clean as I ever desire.* The next day Wesley set out about 4 a.m. and rode to Leadhills, Lesmahagow and reached Glasgow about 8 p.m.

24 June 1766: (Wesley had been travelling from Glasgow) *Before eight (a.m.) we reached Dumfries, and after a short bait(1) we pushed on, in hopes of reaching Solway-Firth before the sea was come in. Designing to call at an inn by the Firth side, we inquired the way, and were directed to leave the main road, and go straight to the house, which we saw before us. In ten minutes Duncan Wright was embogged. However, the horse plunged on, and got through. I was inclined to turn back; but Duncan telling me I needed only go a little to the left, I did so, and sunk at once to my horse's shoulders. He sprung up twice, and twice sunk again, each time deeper than before. At the third plunge he threw me on*

one side, and we both made shift to scramble out. I was covered with fine, soft mud, from my feet to the crown of my head; yet blessed be God, not hurt at all. But we could not cross till between seven and eight o'clock. An honest man crossed with us, who went two miles out of his way to guide us over the sands to Skilborneze(2), where we found a little clean house, and passed a comfortable night. Wesley rode on to Whitehaven.

26 March 1767: (Wesley was coming north from Cumberland). *We rode through miserable roads to Solway-Firth; but the guides were so deeply engaged at a cock-fight, that none could be procured to show us over. We procured one, however, between three and four; but there was more sea than we expected; so that notwithstanding all I could do, my legs and the skirts of my coat were in the water. The motion of the waves made me a little giddy; but it had a stranger effect on Mr. Atlay: he lost his sight, and was just dropping off his horse, when one of our fellow-travellers caught hold of him. We rode on nine or ten miles, and lodged at a village called Ruthwell.*

27 March 1767: *We rode by Dumfries and the Bridge of Urr, over the Military-Way(3), to Gatehouse of Fleet; but the house was filled with such noisy company, that we expected little rest: before eleven, however, I fell asleep, and heard nothing more till between three and four in the morning.*

*The Brow Well and cottages, near Ruthwell from "The Land of Burns" by Professor Wilson, 1841.*

28 March 1767: *We rode to Portpatrick.*

29 March 1767: *The packet-boat was ready in the morning, but waited for the mail, hour after hour, till past three in the afternoon. Hereby we avoided a violent storm, and had only what they called a fresh breeze.*

12 May 1788: (Wesley was travelling into Scotland from Carlisle) *Today we went on through lovely roads to Dumfries. Indeed all the roads are wonderfully mended since I last travelled this way.* (Probably in 1770 when he stayed in an admirable inn at Dumfries). *Dumfries is beautifully situated, but as to wood and water, and gently rising hills, etc. is, I think, the neatest, as well as the most civilized town that I have seen in the kingdom. Robert Dall soon found me out. He has behaved exceeding well, and done much good here. But he is a bold man. He has begun building a preaching-house, larger than any in Scotland, except those in Glasgow and Edinburgh! In the evening I preached abroad in a convenient street, on one side of the town. Rich and poor attended from every quarter, of whatever denomination; and every one seemed to hear for life. Surely the Scots are the best hearers in Europe!*

*Dumfries from above the Dockhead, c.1794.*

14 May 1788: *At five I was importuned to preach in the preaching-house. But such a one I never saw before! It had no windows at all: so that although the sun shone bright, we could see nothing without candles. But I believe our Lord shone on many hearts, while I was applying those words, "I will; be thou clean." I breakfasted with poor Mr. Ashton, many years ago a member of our Society in London, but far happier now in his little cottage, than ever he was in his prosperity.*

*When I was in Scotland first, even at a nobleman's table, we had only flesh-meat of one kind, but no vegetables of any kind: but now they are as plentiful here as in England. Near Dumfries there are five very large public gardens, which furnish the town with greens and fruit in abundance.*

*The congregation in the evening was nearly double to that we had the last, and, if it was possible, more attentive. Indeed one or two gentlemen, so called, laughed at first, but they quickly disappeared, and all were still while I explained, "The worship of God in spirit and in truth.' Two of the Clergy followed me to my lodging, and gave me a pressing invitation to their houses. Several others intended, it seems, to do the same, But having a long journey before me, I left Dumfries earlier in the morning than they expected. We set out on Thursday, the 15th, at four, and reached Glasgow Friday, 16th, before noon. Much of the country as we came is now well improved, and the wilderness become a fruitful field.*

Wesley's last visit to Scotland was in 1790 when he was 86 years old. His Journal for 1 January 1790 recorded: *I am now an old man, decayed from head to foot. My eyes are dim; my right hand shakes much; my mouth is hot and dry every morning. I have a lingering fever almost every day. My motion is weak and slow. However, blessed be God, I do not slack my labour. I can preach and write still.* Despite his weakness he continued his travels, and in the spring visited the north of England and Aberdeen and Glasgow.

31 May 1790: *We set out (from Glasgow) at two, and came to Moffat soon after three in the afternoon. Taking fresh horses, we reached Dumfries between six and seven, and found the congregation waiting; so after a few minutes, I preached on Mark III. 35: "Whosoever doeth the will of God, the same is my brother, and sister, and mother.*

1 June 1790: *Mr. Mather had a good congregation at five. In the day I conversed with many of the people; a candid, humane, well-behaved people, unlike most that I have found in Scotland. In the evening the house was filled, and truly God preached to their hearts. Surely God will have a considerable people here.*

2 June 1790: *We set out early, and reached Carlisle about noon.*

Despite Wesley's efforts there was little sustained interest in Scotland in Methodism. The Scots still preferred to hear well-constructed theological sermons than evangelical fervour.

**NOTES**

1   A bait was a traveller's stop at an inn.

2   Skinburness near Silloth.

3   The Military Road ran from the River Sark to Portpatrick to facilitate the movement of troops between Great Britain and Ireland. From Dumfries it went through Cargenbridge, Lochfoot, Milton, and Haugh of Urr to Carlingwark. Thence to Twynholm and Gatehouse of Fleet. From Anwoth it went over the hills to Creetown. From Newton Stewart it ran to Glenluce and Portpatrick. The section from Dumfries to Creebridge was constructed in 1763-64. As far as possible existing roads were improved but there were deviations and some new bridges. (See the articles in volumes 28 and 72 in the Transactions of the Dumfries and Galloway Natural History and Antiquarian Society).

# BISHOP POCOCKE

Richard Pococke was born in 1704 in Southampton, where his father was a clergyman. He became an Exhibitioner of Corpus Christi College in Oxford and then an Anglican clergyman. Pococke had a passion for travelling and visited Egypt and other lands at the eastern end of the Mediterranean between 1737 and 1742. He published an account of his travels and became known as a celebrated Oriental traveller and author. In 1745 he was appointed Archdeacon of Dublin. Pococke was a strong supporter of the Hanoverian government and rejoiced in the victory at Culloden. In the autumn of 1747 he started his first northern journey, visiting Dunbar, Edinburgh, Glasgow, Kilmarnock and Portpatrick before returning to Ireland. In 1750 he made an extensive tour in the northern counties of England and then crossed over the River Sark on a brief visit to Dumfriesshire. In 1756 he was appointed Bishop of Ossory. In 1760 he carried out a much more lengthy tour of Scotland. He was appointed Bishop of Meath in July 1765 but he died a few weeks later in September 1765.

On 30 April 1760 Pococke landed at Portpatrick and then went to Stranraer - *a small neat town, with an old castle in it. The inhabitants live chiefly by the Herring fishery.* He visited Glenluce Abbey and then passed to Glenluce - *a little town pleasantly situated.* He headed south along the east side of Luce Bay to Glasserton and across to Whithorn. There he examined the Priory. Whithorn, according to Pococke, consisted mostly of farmers and a few tradesmen and manufacturers in woollen and linen for home consumption. On the way to the Isle of Whithorn he saw *they had been digging for coal, and had raised a fine sandy yellow clay, but were obstructed by the water. I could learn no other reason for their sinking for coals, but that it was in the right line from Whitehaven, I suppose north-west. I came to the Isle, which is a little harbour formed by a pier, within which they have 18 feet water at high tides, and a ship of 300 tons can come in. They export barley and import plank and iron from Gothenburg in Sweden, and send it by boats to Wigtown, as the entrance and harbour there are not good. There is a bridge over to the island, under which the sea passes at high water. The principal houses are on the west side of it, and on the Isle near the bridge is a row of poor houses. This part of the Isle is flat, and in high seas the water seems to have come over and divided it from the rising ground beyond it, on which there is a small church. The stones have been taken out of the door and windows… it is probable that this was the ancient Candida Casa(1).*

On 2 May Pococke went to Wigtown which he described as *most delightfully situated on an eminence which commands a view of this river [Cree], the bay, the sea, and all the adjacent coasts of Scotland and England. It consists of one broad street which, about the cross and market house, is like a square, and the houses are tolerable, but below it is narrower, with thatched houses on each side.* He then rode to Newton Stewart, *a neat little town, and there is a fine bridge of four arches over the river.* On the

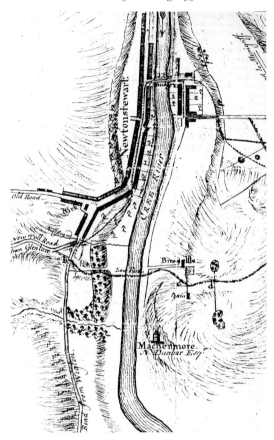

*Newton Stewart and the bridge over the Cree, from a survey by John Gillone, 1809.*

way to Creetown he passed by some holes where they had attempted to find lead. He visited Cardoness Castle, Gatehouse and Tongland where he found that *the abbey is entirely ruined, and great part of it was lately undermined for the sake of the stone.* He noted that there was a considerable salmon fishery at Kirkcudbright and that it was commonly called Kirkoubry. The Bishop then went to Dundrennan, *a small village in which there are most magnificent remains of a fine abbey - the west part is entirely destroyed, except that the Gothic arch on each side leading to the Aisle remains. The east part is standing.*

The Bishop travelled on to Auchencairn. *They found some iron ore about this place, but it did not answer in the smelting. They have also searched for coal at Rascarrel, at a small distance, and propose to carry it on by subscription. This place is near the River Urr, in which they have a bed of oysters, and they catch in the sea cod and mackerel, but they have no herring in this part, as they probably go to the west of the Isle of Man.* He noted that cockle-shells and sea-shells were used for manure.

*They have grouse and the black game on the mountains and abundance of foxes. They have also a wild cat three times as big as the common cat, as the polecat is less. They are of a yellow red colour, their breasts and sides white. They take fowls and lambs, and breed two at a time. I was assured that they sometimes bring forth in a large bird's nest, to be out of the reach of dogs; and it is said they will attack a man who would attempt to take their young ones, but they often shoot them and take the young. The county pays about £20 a year to a person who is obliged to come and destroy the foxes when they send to him.*

Pococke proceeded to Kirkgunzeon and from there by a very rough road and over hills to New Abbey. He described the state of the ruins in some detail. Then he went to Dumfries. *This town carried on a great tobacco trade until the Tobacco Act passed(2), which destroyed that commerce; and the people being grown rich, and their money not employed in trade, they have lately adorned the town with beautiful buildings of the red hewn freestone, and the streets are most exceedingly well paved. They have a handsome Townhouse, and all is kept very clean, so that it is one of the neatest towns in Great Britain, and very pleasantly situated on the Nith, over which there is a large bridge; and, as the Assizes(3) are held here for all the south part of Scotland, the town is much frequented by lawyers. The shipping lie under Criffel, eight miles below Dumfries, and come up three miles higher to unload at Glencaple.*

The Bishop then returned to England. On 8 May they *came over the Sark into England and crossed the Esk with a guide; it being dangerous after high tides, which bring in the sand, and make it very difficult to pass without a guide.* He returned to Scotland in August travelling up Annandale and subsequently went as far north as Kirkwall.

**NOTES**

1   The Candida Casa or White House is associated with St. Ninian (more correctly Nynia). He seems to have been a 5th century bishop who built a church of stone (which appeared to be white) at Whithorn or the Isle of Whithorn. The Priory at Whithorn and the small Chapel on

the Isle - the ruins of both can still be seen - were built in much later times. Very little is known about Nynia, and there is considerable controversy over when he lived and what he did. His reputation may have been built up by the Anglican Church (which spread into the south of Scotland from Northumbria in the 8th century) as a counterpoise to that of St. Columba in the rival Celtic Church.

2   Acts passed in 1722 and 1751 tightened the administration of the Customs. The 1722 Act was a factor in a significant reduction in the tobacco trade in Scotland for some years, but the 1751 Act made less impact on the growth of the trade.

3   Pococke used an English legal term. He should have referred to the Circuits of the High Court Judges.

# THOMAS PENNANT

Thomas Pennant, a Welshman, lived from 1726 to 1798. He was interested in Natural History and in 1767 he was elected to be a Fellow of the Royal Society. In 1771 he published A Tour in Scotland in 1769. On that visit he returned through Moffat and crossed the Sark, but his account of passing through Dumfriesshire was very brief. In the summer of 1772 he returned to Scotland and wrote a further account which was published in 1774. The following extracts are taken from his descriptions of the visit in 1772:

*The town of Langholm appears in a small plain, with the entrance of three dales, and as many rivers, from which they take their names, entering into it, viz. Wauchopedale, Ewesdale and Eskdale; the last extends thirty or forty miles in length, and the sides as far as I could see, bounded by hills of smooth and verdant grass, the sweet food of the sheep, the great staple of the country. To give an idea of the considerable traffic carried on in these animals, the reader may be told, that from twenty to thirty-six thousand lambs are sold in the several fairs that are held in Langholm in the year. To this must be added, the great profit made of the wool, sold into England for our coarser manufactures; of the sheep themselves sent into the south, and even of the cheese and butter made from the milk of the ewes. The manufacturers of Langholm, are stuffs, serges, black and white plaids, plains etc. mostly sold into England.*

*Langholm c.1810.*

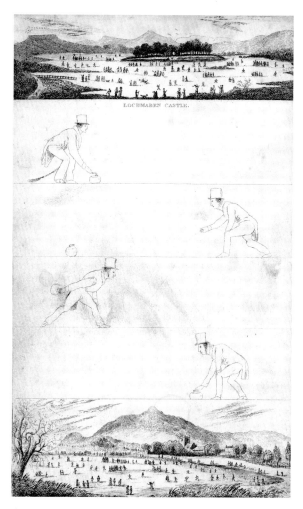

*Curling scenes from Memorabilia Curliana Mabenensis by Richard Broun 1830.*

*The castle is no more than a square tower, or border-house, once belonging to the Armstrongs. In my walk to it was shown the place where several witches had suffered in the last century. …The magistrates of this place are very attentive to the suppression of all excessive exertions of that unruly member the tongue: the Brank, an instrument of punishment, is always in readiness; and I was favoured with the sight: it is a sort of head-piece, that opens and encloses the head of the impatient, while an iron, sharp as a chisel, enters the mouth, and subdues the more dreadful weapon within. This had been used a month before, and as it cut the poor female till blood gushed from each side of her mouth, it would be well that the judges in this case would, before they exert their power again, consider not only the humanity, but the legality of this practice… Of the sports of these parts, that of curling is a favourite; and one unknown in England: it is an amusement of the winter, and played on the ice, by sliding from one mark to another, great stones of forty to seventy pounds weight, of a hemispherical form, with an iron or wooden handle at top. The object of the player is to lay his stone as near to the mark as possible, to guard that of his partner, which had been well laid before, or to strike off that of his antagonist.*

Pennant then returned south of the Border to Netherby and Longtown before again entering Scotland by crossing a small bridge over the Sark. He passed through Gretna and Annan to Ruthwell.

*The salt-makers of Ruthwell merit mention, as their method seems quite local. As soon as the warm and dry weather of June comes on, the sun brings up and incrusts the surface of the sand with salt: at that time they gather the sand to the depth of an inch, carry it out of the reach of the tide, and lay it in round compact heaps, to prevent the salt from being washed away by the rains: they then make a pit eight feet long and three broad, and the same depth, and plaster the inside with clay, that it may hold water, at the bottom they place a layer of peat and turf, and fill the pit with the collected sand: after that they pour water on it: this filters through the sand, and carries the salt with it into a lesser pit, made at the end of the great one: this they boil in small lead pans, and procure a coarse brown salt, very fit for the purposes of salting meat or fish.*

Pennant then visited various places including Ecclefechan and Caerlaverock Castle. He continued his ride *along the coast to the mouth of the Nith, which empties itself into the vast estuary, where the tide flows in so fast on the level sands that a man well mounted would find difficulty to escape, if surprised by it. The view of the opposite side of Criffel, and the other Galloway hills, is very beautiful, and the coast appeared well wooded.* At Glencaple he saw that: *The country on both sides the river is extremely beautiful; the banks decorated with numerous groves and villas, richly cultivated and well enclosed. The farmers show no want of industry: they import, as far as from Whitehaven, lime for manure, to the annual amount of twenty-five hundred pounds, paying at the rate of sixpence for the Winchester bushel (1): they are also so happy as to have great quantities of shell marl in the neighbouring morasses; and are now well rewarded for the use of it: much wheat and barley are at present the fruits of their labour, instead of a very paltry oat, and good hay instead of rushes now clothe their meadows. Dumfries, a very neat and well-built town, seated on the Nith and containing about five thousand souls.(2) It was once possessed of a large share of the tobacco trade, but at present has scarce any commerce. The great weekly markets (3) for black cattle are of much advantage to the place; and vast droves from Galloway and the shire of Ayr pass through in the way to the fairs in Norfolk and Suffolk. The two churches are remarkably neat, and have handsome galleries, supported by pillars.*

From Dumfries he went to Drumlanrig: *In my walks about the park see the white breed of wild cattle, derived from the native race of the country; and still retain the primaeval savageness and ferocity of their ancestors: were more shy than any deer; ran away on the appearance of any of the human species, and even set off at full gallop on the least noise; so that I was under the necessity of going very softly under the shelter of trees or bushes, to get a near view of them: during summer they keep apart from all other cattle, but in severe weather hunger will compel them to visit the out-houses in search of food.*(4) After visiting Morton Castle, Durisdeer and Tibbers Castle, he crossed the Lowther hills by Wanlockhead and went north through Lanark to the Hebrides.

### NOTES

1   Until 1826 the standard bushel was known as the Winchester bushel, as the standard was kept in the town hall at Winchester.

2   Estimated at about 5600 in 1791-92 (Statistical Account of Scotland, 1978 edition, vol. IV, page 130.

3   The Dumfries cattle market held on the Whitesands at the Nith was the main tryst in the South of Scotland in Pennant's time and into the early decades of the 19th century. Dumfries lay in the centre of a substantial cattle-rearing area and also on some of the drove roads to Carlisle and beyond. The cattle were driven into England across the Solway Firth at fords near the mouth of the Esk. If the timing was incorrect, this could result in a disaster with the incoming tide. During the 19th century the driving of cattle (and sheep) declined due to the enclosure of fields curtailing opportunities to feed herds on the move, the breeding of fatter cattle, the advent of steam-ships and then the spread of a network of railways.

4   There is still a herd of wild, white cattle at Drumlanrig.

# JOHN LETTICE

Lettice who was born in 1737 was a poet and clergyman. He was educated at Sidney Sussex College in Cambridge and became a Fellow of the College. In 1794 his 'Letters on a Tour through various parts of Scotland in the year 1792' were published. The account of his visit was written in the style of a series of letters. He crossed into Scotland from Carlisle in August and proceeded north through Lockerbie and Moffat to Glasgow and then into the Highlands. He returned south via Aberdeen, Dundee, Perth and Edinburgh. Lettice died in 1832.

*We entered North Britain by Annandale, in the county of Dumfries: The whole face of the country, on either side of the road to Moffat is hilly, but not mountainous, and, with little exception, appears green. The general scene was pasture; broken up, however, here and there, into potato grounds, and lands of oats and barley. Cottages, ill-built and worse thatched, were thinly scattered about. Farm-houses, in a style even superior to the generality of those more southward, but not numerous, gave relief to our prospects. Cottages sufficiently collected to constitute what we should call a village, or even a hamlet, are rare for many miles. Almost every little dwelling, we saw, has its folding door; not, you will suppose, from any affectation of elegance, which that circumstance sometimes announces with us; but that half the aperture of the common entrance may continue closed, except in cases of necessity, to exclude, as much as possible, the winds and beating rains, to which the western side of Scotland is much subject.*

*At Ecclefechan, a small town through which we passed, famous for its monthly sales of black cattle, the street was full of the peasantry of the neighbourhood; men, women and children making their bargains at the stalls, or otherwise amusing themselves in the afternoon of one of their fair-days; its principal business at this hour being over, and the Cumberland chapmen(1) retired. The Scots bonnet and plaid surtout(2), worn by the men; the short jacket and petticoat of two different colours, and the square checked wrapper or cloak, the covering of the more ordinary women, prevailed in the dress of the elderly people: the younger persons, of both sexes, shone in a tawdry imitation of their southern neighbours. The men's outward dress, or surtout, is a thick stuff of small-checked plaid, blue, or green on a white ground; and is commonly made in the Lowlands, like a rocquelaure(3). It is, unless in bad weather, either drawn up round the middle of the body, or hung negligently over the left shoulder with no ungraceful air.*

*All, that we could further observe, in merely passing through the crowd, was, in general, a shrewd solemnity of visage, not wanting good humour; and, in more juvenile faces, not without simplicity. This last trait, however, amiable as it is, cannot be expected to mark the countenance very strongly after maturer years, among those, whose vocation is minute bargaining.*

*All round Ecclefechan, and for some miles indeed before we reached, as well as after we had passed it, we saw numberless large herds of black cattle and galloways(4), which at this season continually descend from the northern mountains, occupying the pastures on our road's side, and snatching their hasty meal, as they journey to the fairs of South Britain. Each herd is conducted by a Highlander completely dressed in his national garb, accompanied by his brindled(5) dog, of the true shepherd race; as sagacious, docile, and adroit an animal, as retains to the service of man. It is amusing to see something of order and discipline in the movement of eighty, or a hundred head of cattle, under the skilful manoeuvres of a single herdsman and his dog. When the herds are larger, more attendance is allowed for conducting them.*

*Wood being very scarce, and hedge-rows almost unknown in this part of Scotland, walls neatly reared of living sods of earth with alternate layers of stones or pebbles, broad at the bottom, and narrowing to a sharp ridge at the top, form the only enclosure of corn, or pasture lands. Although these walls, from their lowness and precise regularity of form, fail to break the country into those picturesque varieties of shape and colour arising from hedge-rows with large forest trees interspersed, they are infinitely less harsh and unpleasant to the eye, then the naked stone-fences, rough and uncemented, which we saw in the unwooded parts of Westmoreland and Cumberland. Notwithstanding one half of these Annandale fences consists of stone, the verdure of the sod completely covers the whole, a short time after the structure is raised.*

*On the subject of rural economy, as strangers in this country, we could not but observe the practice of setting up their hay in a number of small ricks, each about a cart-load, when the grass is become as dry as the climate will admit of; in order that it may contract the necessary heat, and have time to evaporate it, before the crop is brought home to the thatched in the rick-yard, or deposited under cover for winter's use. In this preparatory state the husbandman suffers it to remain for several weeks. Hay not completely ripened, and seldom got up quite dry, could not at first be gathered into stacks of large bulk without danger of its taking fire. The frequent appearance of these rokes, as they are here called, (although the hay harvest is yet not more than half finished) collected together in one corner of the enclosed fields produces an effect of character on the face of the country remarkable to a stranger, and by no means disagreeable. This practice, which we understand, to prevail throughout all North Britain, has arisen undoubtedly from the nature of a climate subject to such degrees of cold or humidity, as prevent the crops from ripening sufficiently to be cut, before the summer is far advanced; if indeed they can often be said to arrive at perfect maturity.*

Lettice then rode on to the *little market-town* of Lockerbie. At the inn *a poor woman with her young family, opposite our window, attracted our notice, as they were removing within doors a load of turfs, shot from the street. The joyous shrugs and comic gestures of the young ones, their skipping and capering about the heap of fuel, succeeded by a very lively and nimble application of hands, arms, fire-shovels and broken-platters to the business of carrying it within, and, at the conclusion, a thrifty sweeping of the smallest particles that had crumbled from the turf, convinced us how acceptable, even indifferent fuel is in a cold country, and how doubly welcome to those, who, with difficulty, find means to procure any at all. It was impossible not to partake the gladness of this humble scene. I should not, however, have thought it worth describing, though I fear the poverty which it announces may be classed among the characteristics of the place and its vicinage, had I not considered it as another proof of the opinion, you have always strenuously maintained, that the acquisition of the bare necessaries of life causes greater happiness to such as are scarcely able to obtain them, than the enjoyment of the highest luxuries to those, who seem to command the world at their will…*

MOFFAT.

*Moffat, c.1840.*

*After we had left Lockerbie behind, we found ourselves upon an excellent road, and in a district not ill-cultivated, considering its thin population. When we were advanced about ten miles, the road, which ran on the declivity of some lofty wild hills, affording pasture for sheep and much cover for game, commanded, on our left, a succession of pleasant meadows, with a trout stream meandering through them, overhung, on the side opposite to us, by a beautifully wooded shore and green projecting banks reflected from the water….*

*We reached the town (Moffat), consisting of houses not ill-built, but all turned with their gable ends to a large pleasant area; the market place. Cottages of meaner construction running in a line with these superior edifices, and forming streets behind them, make up the town; a place of some bustle on various accounts. The poorer people are employed in manufacturing coarse woollen stuffs, chiefly plaids of small chequer work; of more elegant and less glaring patterns than those made in the Highlands. The better order of inhabitants are partly supported by disposing of the produce of the loom, and partly by letting accommodation to invalids; the rheumatic, the scrofulous, the hypochondriac, or the idle; the last most numerous of the three. Indeed without this useful tribe, with whom all waters agree, though their case is helpless, few of these places would prosper. But the principal movement of the town of Moffat, during our short stay in it, arose, as we understood, it generally does, from the continual passage of travellers to and from Glasgow, Edinburgh, Dumfries, etc. who keep a large inn very much alive both day and night. The many successive arrivals and departures of various rank and figure, in carriages, on horseback or on foot, the constant scene before our window, helped considerably to cheer a very dark and rainy day. We had frequent occasion to admire the unconcerned hardiness of idle spectators, and of persons stopping each other in the market place, to converse during the heaviest showers of rain. Women too, and some not of the lowest class, without hat or bonnet, we saw in conversations tête-à-tête, discovering with as much earnestness, as if perfectly insensible of the weather. These good people unaffected and unhurt by a humid and inclement atmosphere, and remarkable, I may add too, for bearing with indifference, sudden transitions from heat to cold, enjoy, in these respects, an enviable advantage over ourselves. Though no people love better to be warm and snug in their houses and cottages, than the North Britons, no other in Europe perhaps will be found, who meet the severest cold with more patience and resolution.*

**NOTES**

1   A chapman is a pedlar going from place to place selling small articles.

2   A surtout is a man's long overcoat.

3   A rocquelaure is a man's knee-length coat with a cape collar. It was fashionable in the 18th century.

4   Galloways are hornless cattle with rough, glossy, black coats.

5   A grey or tawny coat, streaked or spotted with a darker colour.

# THE 19TH CENTURY

The momentum of material progress was maintained during the 19th century. The south-west, however, remained essentially an agricultural community. The rise of heavy industry which changed much of the west of Scotland so radically was not repeated in the south-west. Attempts in the late 18th century to set up a cotton industry, especially in Gatehouse of Fleet, did not survive for long. There was also industrial development in Maxwelltown on the west side of the Nith opposite Dumfries, but the Dumfries area did not become a major industrial centre.

One result of the lack of industrial employment was a slower relative rise in the population of the three counties compared with some other Scottish counties. The total rose from 106,726 in a total Scottish population of 1,608,420 (6.6%) in 1801 to only 144,639 out of 4,472,103 (3.2%) in 1901.

Although the south-west did not see the growth of industrial conurbations and no large cities emerged there, it became increasingly important to provide certain amenities in the larger towns. Kirkcudbright had led the way in 1763 with a supply of piped water. Lighting by gas was introduced to Dumfries in the late 1820s for the streets and most of the public buildings, but an Act of Parliament to arrange a piped water supply was not obtained until 1850, after two disastrous cholera outbreaks.

Significant changes were also taking place in the countryside. The New Statistical Account for the parish of Kirkmaiden in the Mull of Galloway written in 1839 stated succinctly that 'the most striking variations betwixt the present state of the parish, and that which existed at the time of the last Statistical Account (compiled in 1790), are observable in the introduction of the modern system of husbandry; the most extensive cultivation of green crops, especially potatoes; the substitution of wheat for bear (a form of barley); and the now improved state of the roads.'

There were dramatic improvements in travelling during the course of the century(1). Some improvements to the roads had been made in the second half of the 18th century with the introduction of trusts responsible for stretches of road and levying tolls to meet the costs. There are references to turnpike gates and houses in Dorothy Wordsworth's diary for 19 August 1803 and 28 September

1822. Roads, however, lacked proper surfaces until McAdam (1756-1836) and Telford (1757-1834) introduced top layers of stone chippings. Both had links with the south-west of Scotland. McAdam's ancestors had been granted lands in 1569 in the parish of Carsphairn in the Stewartry. He himself was born in Ayr. For much of his life he worked in England, but he frequently visited Scotland and on such a visit died at Moffat. Telford was born at Westerkirk in Eskdale and was apprenticed to a stonemason in Lochmaben and then in Langholm. In 1782 he went to England and soon received a series of important commissions in civil engineering. He was involved in projects throughout Britain. Robert Southey, the poet, accompanied him in 1819 on a visit to his projects in Scotland. Telford's work in the south-west of Scotland included several bridges (such as the bridge over the River Dee at Tongland) and the remaking of the Glasgow-Carlisle road through Annandale.

The gradual improvement in the roads encouraged the use of stage-coaches and mail-coaches. Frequent services were introduced between cities and towns(2). The network led to extensive employment for those providing changes of horses, but the horses had to endure great hardship and many died from exhaustion. Journeys could still be dangerous as roads were not lit, and the coaches had only lamps. Deep snow and floods were further hazards. The age of the coach was portrayed in Scott's 'The Antiquary' and John Buchan's 'The Free Fishers.'

Sea-borne traffic on the Solway was boosted by the introduction of steam-ships. For some decades in the mid 19th century the harbours on the Solway were busy with coastal trade. In the 1830s a steam-boat service was started once a week during the summer between Dumfries and Whitehaven, and there were regular steam-packets from Annan to Liverpool. In the 1840s there were regular services by steam-packet to Liverpool from Kirkcudbright, Wigtown and Carsethorn. James Wilson's account shows the influence of the steam-ship on the various Wigtownshire harbours.

The stage-coaches and subsequently some of the steam-ships gradually disappeared following the opening of railway lines in the south-west starting in the late 1840s. The development of a network of railway lines by various companies made access to the south-west much easier for visitors. There were both main and local lines. Access was provided to towns across the south-west such as Portpatrick, Stranraer, Wigtown, Whithorn, Kirkcudbright, Castle Douglas, Moniaive, Dumfries, Moffat and Langholm. Despite the network of railways the south-west was a little too far from major centres of population for the growth of any major holiday resorts.

**NOTES**

1   One of the most important was the construction of a bridge over the Esk. See Cobbett's account.

2   Dumfries had regular services to Edinburgh, Glasgow and London. The article by J. M. Corrie on the Dumfries Post Office, 1642-1910 in the Transactions of the Dumfries and Galloway Natural History and Antiquarian Society for 1911-12 has a section on the Period of the Mail coach, and in TDGNHAS for 1975 there is an article by W. A. J. Prevost on Moffat and Beattock Inn, Two Mail-Coach Stages.

# DOROTHY WORDSWORTH

Dorothy lived from 1771 to 1855 and was the sister of the poet William Wordsworth. She herself is renowned as a notable diarist. In August 1803 she set out on the tour of Scotland from Keswick in the company of her brother and their friend Samuel Coleridge, another famous poet. The Wordsworths had been brought up in the Lake District and took great pleasure in the beauty of the natural world. Unlike many of the earlier visitors to Scotland they appreciated the mountain grandeur of much of the Scottish scenery. The diary which Dorothy kept on her tour was intended not for publication but for her own private circle. The record therefore sets out freely her reactions and feelings. It was published in 1874 as 'Recollections of a Tour made in Scotland A.D. 1803.' The travellers passed through Nithsdale and crossed the Lowther Hills by Wanlockhead to Crawfordjohn. After visiting Glasgow they entered the Highlands through the Vale of Leven. They travelled extensively in the Southern Highlands, visiting Inveraray, Appin, Glen Coe, Loch Tummel, Dunkeld and the Trossachs. On their return journey they went to Edinburgh, Melrose, Hawick and Langholm and on 24 September crossed into England.

*Dorothy Wordsworth*

17 August

*We enter Scotland by crossing the river Sark; on the Scotch side of the bridge the ground is unenclosed pasturage; it was very green, and scattered over with that yellow flowered plant which we call grunsel; the hills heave and swell prettily enough; cattle feeding; a few corn fields near the river. At the top of the hill opposite is Springfield(1), a village built by Sir William Maxwell - a dull uniformity in the houses, as is usual when all built at one time, or belonging to one individual, each just big enough for two people to live in, and in which a family, large or small as it may happen, is crammed. There the marriages are performed. Further on, though almost contiguous, is Gretna Green, upon a hill and among trees. This sounds well, but it is a dreary place; the stone houses dirty and miserable, with broken windows. There is a pleasant view from the churchyard over Solway firth to the Cumberland mountains. Dined at Annan. On our left as we travelled along appeared the Solway firth and the mountains beyond, but the near country dreary. Those houses by the roadside which are built of stone are comfortless and dirty; but we peeped into a clay 'biggin' that was very 'canny', and I dare say will be as warm as a swallow's nest in winter. The town of Annan made me think of France and Germany; many of the houses large and gloomy, the size of them outrunning the comforts. One thing which was like Germany pleased me: the shopkeepers express their calling by some device or painting; bread-bakers have biscuits, loaves, cakes painted on their window-shutters; blacksmiths horses' shoes, iron tools etc., and so on through all trades.*

*River Annan from the bridge, c.1830.*

*Reached Dumfries about nine o'clock - market day; met crowds of people on the road and every one had a smile for us and our car(2). The inn was a large house, and tolerably comfortable.*

### 18th August

*Went to the churchyard where Burns is buried(3). A bookseller accompanied us. He showed us the outside of Burns's house, where he had lived the last three years of his life, and where he died. It has a mean appearance, and is in a bye situation, whitewashed; dirty about the doors, as almost all Scotch houses are; flowering plants in the windows.*

*Went on to visit his grave. He lies at a corner of the churchyard, and his second son, Francis Wallace, beside him. There is no stone to mark the spot; but a hundred guineas have been collected, to be expended on some sort of monument.*

*When our guide had left us, we turned again to Burns's house. Mrs. Burns was gone* to spend some time by the sea-shore with her children. We spoke to the servant-maid at the door, who invited us forward, and we sat down in the parlour. The walls were coloured with a blue wash; on one side of the fire was a mahogany desk, opposite to the window a clock, and over the desk a print from the 'Cotter's Saturday Night,' which Burns mentions in one of his letters having received as a present. The house was cleanly and neat in the inside, the stairs of stone, scoured white, the kitchen on the right side of the passage, the parlour on the left. In the room above the parlour the Poet died, and his son after him in the same room.

Travelled through the vale of Nith, here little like a vale, it is so broad, with irregular hills rising up on each side, in outline resembling the old-fashioned valances(4) of a bed. There is a great deal of arable land; the corn ripe; trees here and there - plantations, clumps, coppices, and a newness in everything. So much of the gorse and broom, rooted out that you wonder why it is not all gone, and yet there seems to be almost as much gorse and broom as corn; and they grow one among another you know not how. Crossed the Nith; the vale becomes narrow, and very pleasant; corn fields, green hills, clay cottages; the river's bed rocky, with woody banks. Left the Nith about a mile and a half, and reached Brownhill(5), a lonely inn, where we slept.

William and I walked out after dinner; Coleridge was not well, (he returned to England on 29 August due to his health - Ed.) and slept upon the carriage cushions. We made our way to the cottages among the little hills and knots of wood, and then saw what a delightful country this part of Scotland might be made by planting forest trees. The ground all over heaves and swells like a sea; but for miles there are neither trees nor hedgerows, only 'mound' fences and tracts(6); or slips of corn, potatoes, clover - with hay between, and barren land; but near the cottages many hills and hillocks covered with wood. We passed some fine trees, and paused under the shade of one close by an old mansion that seemed from its neglected state to be inhabited by farmers. But I must say that many of the 'gentleman's' houses which we have passed in Scotland have an air of neglect, and even of desolation.

19 August
Open country for a considerable way. Passed through the village of Thornhill, built by the Duke of Queensberry, the 'brother-houses' so small that they might have been built to stamp a character of insolent pride on his own huge mansion of Drumlanrigg, which is full in view on the opposite side of the Nith. This mansion is indeed very large; but to us it appeared like a gathering together of little things. The roof is broken into a hundred pieces, cupolas, etc., in the shape of casters, conjuror's balls, cups, and the like. The situation would be noble if the woods had been left standing; but they have been cut down not long ago, and the hills above and below the house are quite bare. About a mile and a

*Drumlanrig Castle from Carronbridge, 1845 from a wash drawing by J. Watson of Dumfries.*

*half from Drumlanrigg is a turnpike gate at the top of a hill. We left our car with the man, and turned aside into a field where we looked down upon the Nith, which runs far below in a deep and rocky channel; the banks woody; the view pleasant down the river towards Thornhill, an open country - corn fields, pastures, and scattered trees. Returned to the turnpike house, a cold spot upon a common, black cattle feeding close to the door. Our road led us down the hill to the side of the Nith, and we travelled along its banks for some miles. Here were clay cottages perhaps every half or quarter of a mile. The bed of the stream rough with rocks; banks irregular, now woody, now bare; here a patch of broom, there of corn, then of pasturage; and hills green or heathy above. We were to have given our horse meal and water at a public-house in one of the hamlets we passed through, but missed the house, for, as is common in Scotland, it was without a sign-board. Travelled on, still beside the Nith, till we came to a turnpike house, which stood rather high on the hill-side, and from the door we looked a long way up and down the river. The air coldish, the wind strong. Soon after leaving the turnpike house we turned up a hill to the right, the road for a little way very steep, bare hills, with sheep.*

*When, after a steep ascent, we had reached the top of the hill, we saw a village (Wanlockhead - Ed.) about half a mile before us on the side of another hill, which rose up above the spot where we were, after a descent, a sort of valley or hollow. Nothing grew upon this ground, or the hills above or below, but heather, yet round about the village - which consisted of a great number of huts, all alike, and all thatched, with a few larger slated houses among them, and a single modern-built one of a considerable size - were a hundred patches of cultivated ground, potatoes, oats, hay, and grass. We were struck with the sight of haycocks fastened down with aprons, sheets, pieces of sacking - as we supposed, to prevent the wind from blowing them away. We afterwards found that this practice was very general in Scotland. Every cottage seemed to have its little plot of ground, fenced by a ridge of earth; this plot contained two or three different divisions, kail, potatoes, oats, hay; the houses all standing in lines, or never far apart, the cultivated ground was all together also, and made a very strange appearance with its many greens among the dark brown hills, neither tree nor shrub growing; yet the grass and the potatoes looked greener than elsewhere, owing to the bareness of the neighbouring hills; it was indeed a wild and singular spot.*

23 September (on the return journey going south)

*Arrived at Langholm at about five o'clock. The town, as we approached, from a hill, looked very pretty, the houses being roofed with blue slates, and standing close to the river Esk, here a large river, that scattered its waters wide over a stony channel. The inn neat and comfortable - exceedingly clean: I could hardly believe we were still in Scotland.*

In 1822 Dorothy made a second tour of Scotland(7) passing through Langholm and Mosspaul on her way to Hawick. On her return journey southwards she travelled with her friend Joanna Hutchinson to Elvanfoot(8) and then to a lonely toll-bar about six miles from Moffat. They were welcomed at the turnpike house and stayed the night here. They slept uneasily as they were anxious in case two rough travellers who had stopped at the house would be re-admitted and then murder them. Dorothy recorded in her Journal for 28 September: *We rose at seven, sunshine on the hills; frosty dew, all round the house, black cattle pasturing. Departed at eight, with feelings towards those kind people at the Toll-bar the more friendly for the injustice our fears had done them. The air bright and keen - we ascend from the Dell, our road leading us over the heights spotted with sheep - stream glittering below to the right. No cottages. After four miles walking, Moffat seen at a distance in the valley below - very pretty - spire and silver smoke - green meadows - ripe corn and stubble grounds - new plantations - a want of natural wood, but the lively sunshine making amends for all that would be dreary under a cloudy sky. A continental dullness at Moffat - well-built stone houses - wide street and grass growing on the pavement. Breakfasted at the Inn, large rooms, well furnished but growing shabby - no business. The coaches now stopping at a new Inn, and the new road avoiding the town. Walked to the Well - pretty glen - shabby bathing house.*

**NOTES**

1   Springfield is close to Gretna Green. Sir William began to develop it in 1791. It also became involved in clandestine marriages.

2   A car at that time was an Irish gig.

3   Burns died in 1796. He was buried in the north corner of the cemetery at St. Michael's Church, initially with a simple stone slab. A subscription list was subsequently opened for the erection of a mausoleum. The work was started in 1815 in the south-east corner of the cemetery and the body was transported there with as much privacy as possible very early one morning. The mausoleum was completed in 1819.

4   A valance is a short curtain or drapery hanging from the edge of a bed often to the floor.

5   Brownhill is on the west side of the Nith south-east of Penpont and west of Closeburn.

6   A tract is a continuous expanse of land.

7   The Journals of Dorothy Wordsworth edited by E. de Selincourt (1941), vol. 2, contains her Journal of the 1822 tour.

8   Elvanfoot is on the A702 close to the main Glasgow - Carlisle railway line and the M74 and about 3 miles north-west of Beattock summit.

# SIR WALTER SCOTT

*Sir Walter Scott*

Scott (1771-1832) wrote two novels - Guy Mannering and Redgauntlet - in which most of the action takes place in Dumfries and Galloway; and two novels - Old Mortality and The Abbot - in which there are also south-west settings for part of the action. The plots of two more novels - The Heart of Midlothian and The Bridge of Lammermoor - derive from south-west origins. Scott's little-known play, The Doom of Devorgoil, also has a setting in Galloway.

According to the biography(1) of Scott written by his son-in-law, J. G. Lockhart, Scott visited Galloway in March 1793 in connection with a case before the General Assembly in which he was defending the Minister of Girthon (which is near Gatehouse of Fleet). This may have been his only visit to Galloway. In 1878 an anonymous correspondent in the Galloway Gazette(2) asserted that Mr. McCulloch of Ardwall (whose sister had married Scott's brother Thomas) had stated that Scott despite repeated invitations was never in Galloway. Possibly that just meant he never visited Ardwall and does not refute Lockhart's reference to a visit in 1793.(3)

Although there is uncertainty over Sir Walter's personal acquaintance with Galloway, he was very familiar with Liddesdale; starting in 1792 he visited Liddesdale for seven years in succession. Some of the best episodes in Guy Mannering stemmed from those visits, but the few surviving details of Scott's visits are those related by his companion, Robert Shortreed. These jaunts were lively, good-natured occasions with Scott laughing and singing.

On several occasions Sir Walter visited Drumlanrig Castle. In September 1813 he recorded that he had been *for a fortnight at Drumlanrig, a grand old chateau, which has descended, by the death of the late Duke of Queensberry, to the Duke of Buccleuch (the head of the Scotts). It is really a most magnificent pile, and when embosomed amid the wide forest scenery, of which I have an infantine recollection, must have been very romantic. But old Q made wild devastation among the noble trees, although some fine ones are still left, and a quantity of young shoots are, in despite of the want of every kind of attention, rushing up to supply the places of the fathers of the forest from whose stems they are springing. It will now I trust be in better hands.*

There had certainly been a transformation by August 1826. Scott recorded on a brief stay at Drumlanrig: *What visions does not this magnificent old house bring back to me! The exterior is much improved since I first knew it. It was then in the state of dilapidation to which it had been abandoned by the celebrated old Q -, and was indeed scarce wind and water tight. Then the whole wood had been felled, and the outraged castle stood in the midst of waste and desolation, excepting a few scattered old stumps, not judged worth the cutting. Now, the whole has been, ten or twelve years since, completely replanted, and the scattered seniors look as graceful as fathers surrounded by their children. The face of this immense estate has been scarcely less wonderfully changed. The scrambling tenants, who held a precarious tenure of lease under the Duke of Queensberry, at the risk (as actually took place) of losing their possession at his death, have given room to skilful men, working their farms regularly, and enjoying comfortable houses, at a rent which is enough to forbid idleness, but not to overpower industry.* A few days later Scott departed

*The Grey Mare's Tail from Fairfoul's Guide to Moffat, 2nd edition, 1879.*

from Drumlanrig to return home to Abbotsford. On the journey: *we viewed the Grey Mare's Tail, and I still feel confident in crawling along the ghastly bank, by which you approach the fall.*

In 1805 there had also been a visit to the Grey Mare's Tail. Scott had made a memorable excursion from his house at Ashestiel near the Tweed in Selkirkshire into the wild countryside north of Moffat. There are two descriptions of this visit: one by James Skene in his Memories of Sir Walter Scott and the other by James Hogg in his Domestic Manners of Sir Walter Scott.

Skene was born in 1775 and came from Rubislaw near Aberdeen. In 1797 he was admitted to the Scottish Bar. Both Skene and Scott held commissions in the Edinburgh Light Horse and became close friends. Skene visited Scott frequently at Ashestiel and later at Abbotsford. Skene's account of the excursion in 1805 is as follows: *Having been to visit the wild scenery of the hills above Moffat, remarkable for the cascade of the Grey Mare's Tail; and the dark mountain tarn, called Loch Skene* (now Skeen)*, we had just got bewildered by the thick fog which generally envelopes the wild and rugged features of that lonely scene, and in groping our way among the bogs and black peat hags, the ground gave way, and down we went, horsemen, horses and all, into a slough of peaty mud and black water, out of which, entangled as we were with our plaids and our prostrate nags, it was not easy to extricate ourselves. We had prudently left our own horses at a farmhouse below, and got the use of the farmer's hill ponies for the occasion; otherwise the result might have been serious. As it was we rose like the spirits of the bog, covered with slime; to free themselves from this our ponies rolled about among the heather, and we had nothing for it but to follow their example. We finally reached the loch, and saw an eagle rise majestically from its margin. One cannot well imagine a more desolate and savage scene than that part of Loch Skene, particularly as it then presented itself, partially disclosed from under the thick folds of fog that rolled over its surface; suddenly caught by an occasional gust of wind the fog was rent asunder, giving for a moment some more distant portion to view, then closing again and opening in some other quarter, so as at one time to show a projecting rocky point, at another an island with a few blighted trees and the cheerless scene of hags and heath in which it lay. Much of the scenery in the tale of Old Mortality was drawn from the recollection of this day's ride. We got down to Moffat, and thence returned by Ettrick Water.* (It would be interesting to know the precise route of that return journey).

James Hogg (1770-1835), poet and novelist, and known as the 'Ettrick Shepherd' was primarily a sheep farmer. He had received hardly any formal education but read widely and began to write poems. In 1802 he met Sir Walter and their friendship, at times a little strained, continued for many years. Hogg's account of the excursion is as follows: *I remember leaving my own cottage here one morning with him, accompanied by my dear friend, William Laidlaw, and Sir Adam Ferguson, to visit the tremendous solitudes of Loch Skene and the Grey-Mare's-Tail. I conducted them through that wild region by a path, which, if not rode by Clavers* (Claverhouse was one of the persecutors of the Covenanters in the 17th century)*, as reported, never was rode by another gentleman. Sir Adam rode inadvertently into a gulf and got a sad fright, but Sir Walter, in the very worst paths, never dismounted, save at Loch Skene to take some dinner. We went to Moffat that night, where we met with Lady Scott and Sophia* (Scott's eldest child)*, and such a day and night of glee I never witnessed. Our very perils were to him matter of infinite merriment; and then there was a short tempered boot-boy at the inn, who wanted to pick a quarrel with him for some of his sharp retorts, at which Scott laughed till the water ran over his cheeks.*

*I was disappointed in never seeing some incident in his subsequent works laid in a scene resembling the rugged solitude around Loch Skene, for I never saw him survey any with so much attention. A single serious look at a scene generally filled his mind with it, and he seldom took another. But, here, he took the names of all the hills, their altitudes, and relative situations with regard to one another, and made me repeat all these several times. Such a scene may occur in some of his works which I have not seen, and I think it will, for he has rarely ever been known to interest himself either in a scene or a character, which did not appear afterwards in all its most striking peculiarities.*

It is interesting to note that Hogg, unlike Skene, did not detect a similarity to what they had seen that day in one of the closing scenes in 'Old Mortality'. Hogg knew that novel as he considered the joint key-stones of Scott's prose were 'Old Mortality' and 'Guy Mannering.'

**NOTES**

1  J. G. Lockhart's Memoirs of Sir Walter Scott, chapter VII.

2  Galloway Gazette for 4th May, 1878.

3  P. H. McKerlie in 'Galloway in Ancient and Modern Times.' (1891) page 308 stated that Scott had told his friend Mr. Joseph Train that 'neither had he visited Galloway further than being once in Gatehouse on professional business.'

# RICHARD AYTON

Ayton was born in London in 1786. His father was a banker in Lombard Street. Subsequently the family moved to Macclesfield in Cheshire. For a time he studied law, but when he reached the age of 21 he retired to the coast of Sussex and amused himself according to his own wishes. His special delight was boating. In 1813 he started a journey round Britain, reaching the Solway in the summer of 1814. His companion was William Daniell, a landscape painter. An account of the journey entitled 'A Voyage round Great Britain' began to appear in 1814. There were several volumes and Daniell contributed the illustrations. Ayton subsequently became a playwright but achieved little success. His health deteriorated and he died in London in 1823.

Ayton and Daniell had originally intended to travel principally by sea, but the plan was found to be utterly impracticable. As they wished to examine every point and cranny of the coast, only a small rowing-boat could have been considered, but it could not have coped with 'rapid tides, ground-swells, insurmountable surfs, strong winds, and foul winds.' So the two 'navigators' frequently 'sailed' on horseback or 'scudded along' in a gig.

Ayton was certainly a percipient observer and a good author. At times, however, his remarks about the Scots and their living conditions were rather blunt and offensive. The following extracts are taken from some of his more judicious and less scathing passages:

*As Annan was the first town that I had the pleasure of seeing in Scotland, I entered it with some curiosity, looking out narrowly for its peculiar marks and distinctions. It is very agreeably situated on an eminence above a fertile valley, watered by the Annan, which, about a mile to the southward, discharges itself into the Solway. The town contains eighteen hundred inhabitants, and consists principally of one broad unpaved street, headed at one end by the gaol with a tower and spire, and flanked on each side by respectable houses and shops, of various elevations, and jutting out in various degrees of projection, with here and there a hut amongst them, not more wretched, I can scarcely think, than some other huts that I have seen, but singular from their being permitted to take their places in the great street. They are built with unhewn stones thrown together as if by accident, and covered with a thatched roof black with rottenness, but giving nourishment to a harvest of rank grass and weeds, and topped by most uncouth chimneys, each formed by four stakes placed about a foot asunder, and wrapped round with bands of straw, or filled up with sods of earth.*

Ayton was quite complimentary about the school he visited in Annan:

*The parish schools, justly the boast of Scotland, formed interesting subjects of inquiry and observation to me during my tour in the country. I was pleased at seeing here for the first time, a room full of dirty, ragged boys, some learning English, some Latin, and some arithmetic, and all obviously in earnest and attentive to their tasks, from a proper reverence for their respectable teacher.*

He proceeded to Dumfries. The High Street there displays *a stateliness suited to a town of this rank and importance, it is of a fine breadth, with houses and shops on each side of a magnitude, beauty and elegance, that would do credit to any town in the kingdom. The eye is offended by the awkward situation of the town-hall, which stands plump in the middle of the street, interfering materially with the beauty of its perspective, and not a little with its commodiousness as a thoroughfare. There are several other very good streets, one in particular of great elegance, called Buccleugh street, but just finished, and not yet*

Drawn by A.S. Masson                          Engd by John Gellatly.

*Buccleuch Street, Dumfries, 1832 from:- "A Pictorial History of Dumfries and its Environs" by John McDiarmid.*

*inhabited. Dumfries, like all the towns of any consequence in Scotland, is built of stone, which adds much to the beauty and dignity of its appearance. I strayed into one or two miserable alleys, and observed that some of the better streets, with their modern improvements, were deformed by the unseemly intervention of some of the ancient huts.* Ayton also commented on the changes in the village of Maxwelltown across the River Nith: *the houses have been thoroughly cleansed inside and out, and are neat and* decent; and the people having under-gone the same operation, have become sober, quiet and industrious.

He then headed for the Stewartry, passing through New Abbey, Carsethorn, Southerness and Auchencairn to Dundrennan. His supper there *consisted of barley-broth, served up in a brown earthenware basin, with a great horn-spoon in it, the bowl of which might have visited the capacious mouth of a shark.* Ayton visited Dundrennan Abbey and Port Mary House which opened *in front into a semicircular bay,* and passed this bay. He arrived at Port Mary and reflected on the departure of Mary Queen of Scots from it. He then walked from the creek along the side of the Abbey burn which *from Dundrennan to the sea flows through a very pretty glen, thickly planted with oak trees*(1).

Ayton continued westward along the line of the coastal cliffs(2): *I had seldom seen a more striking display of the untamed magnificence of nature: here was the ocean in all its grandeur, ploughed up by a storm, and bursting with a continued and sullen roar against precipices of rock, awful from their vastness, black and dreadful, and exposing on their battered sides a combination of all rugged and horrid forms.* He rounded Torrs Point and witnessed a scene of an entirely altered character and *one of extraordinary beauty. The fine expanse of the Dee before me was forked by St. Mary's Isle, so entirely covered with wood, that it looked like a grave rising from the water: beyond it the river was lost to the sight amidst closing hills, with their summits crowned with woods, and their sloping sides adorned by corn fields and meadows - a fairy land indeed, compared with the rough and naked wastes which still bordered the shore to my right.*

Ayton arrived at Kirkcudbright, which he described as *a very small town, consisting principally of two short streets, neat, clean and quiet, without manufactures, and with very limited commercial relations beyond its own immediate vicinity.* On the day of his arrival *the town was in a state of amazing bustle and agitation, with music playing, colours flying, and nearly all the men of the place pacing in procession through the principal street.* It was the day for the election of the Deacons of trades.

Gatehouse of Fleet was described by Ayton as *a large village, remarkable for the neatness and regularity of its streets and houses. The main street is spacious and well paved, and the houses on each side of it are of good size and very compact, mostly white-washed, and roofed with slates. At one extremity this street is connected with a handsome bridge, which, on the opposite side of the river, leads into another street equally neat and clean.* He found *a very jolly and turbulent party assembled at the inn in Gatehouse, compared of riders or bag-men, as they are called, an order of itinerant trades. They have a room set apart for them in every inn, called the travellers room hung round with coats and whips, filled in every corner with bags and bundles.*

The famous 19th century historian, Thomas Carlyle, who was born at Ecclefechan in Annandale in 1795, told Queen Victoria that he believed there was no finer or more beautiful drive in her kingdom than the one round the shore of the Stewartry by Gatehouse of Fleet(3). Ayton was also enthusiastic about this road: *The whole stage between Gatehouse and Creetown, at the head of Wigton Bay, has been stated to be one of the finest rides in Scotland, and, as far as my observation has extended, I am not disposed to think that such signal praise is unmeasured and undeserved.*

*Portpatrick, 1813 from Daniell and Ayton's, "A Voyage Round Great Britain."*

Ayton proceeded through Wigtownshire to Portpatrick. He recorded that: *The town is small, and thrives but slowly, as is generally the case with thoroughfares of this kind. It is chiefly supported by the constant concourse of passengers by the packets, who here find accommodation according to their circumstances, almost every house being an inn.*

**NOTES**

1   Ayton's account shows very clearly that at the time of his visit the creek at the Abbey Burnfoot was called Port Mary, and that the bay to the east in front of Port Mary House at that time was not called Port Mary.

2   In recent years these cliffs are within the M.O.D. range.

3   See John Ruskin's Praeterita, vol. III, section 64.

# JOHN KEATS

*John Keats.*

Keats, who was born in 1795 and died at the age of 26 in 1821, was another famous English poet who visited Dumfries and Galloway. In the summer of 1818 he went on a walking tour through the Lake District and Scotland with his friend Charles Brown.

At the beginning of July they arrived at Dumfries. Keats wrote in a letter: *Yesterday was an immense Horse fair at Dumfries, so that we met numbers of men and women on the road, the women nearly all barefoot, with their shoes and clean stockings in hand, ready to put on and look smart in the Towns.* At Dumfries they visited Burns' tomb in the churchyard corner and also went to visit the ruins at Lincluden. Then they proceeded through Galloway. Keats wrote *we are in the midst of Meg Merrilees' country of whom I suppose you have heard*(1). He considered Kirkcudbrightshire as *very beautiful, very wild with craggy hills somewhat in the Westmoreland fashion.*

Regrettably Keats' account of the journey is too often marred by frivolous and flippant comments, and consequently there is little worth quoting from his letters. Fortunately his companion was much more gifted at describing the countryside they saw. From Dumfries they went across country to Dalbeattie and consequently missed seeing New Abbey. The following accounts of their journey are taken from Charles Brown's Journal.

*We had been recommended to seek entertainment at the village of Dalbeattie from a Mr. Murray. Besides keeping a Public, he kept a shop below, supplying every one in the district with almost every article from tea down to candles and brick dust, ironmongery of all sorts, whiskey, broad cloth, sheeting, printed cottons, pens, ink and paper. It was a day appointed by the Kirk for a fast in the parish; and, therefore, the shop was shut, and Mrs. Murray only at home. From some unexplained cause, she was at first unwilling to* let us enter - she *"didna ken what to say!"* Such doubts sound cruelly in the ears of hungry travellers, and should be visited with a grievous penalty. A saunter through the village was pleasant, as the cottages were neat, clean, and snug-looking. Then the inhabitants whom we saw were very clean and healthy faced, and every one of the children was dressed tidily - possibly this was partly owing to its being a holiday, but, even then, it was a credit to the village.

In the evening Mr. Murray conversed with the travellers and gave them the route for going on the next day to Kirkcudbright. He told them that Dalbeattie *did not exist thirty years ago; at that time it was a bog full of rocky stones. The gentleman who built it died the very day I had my leg cut off.* Suddenly they realised he had a wooden leg.

The travellers proceeded to Auchencairn which Brown described as a delightful village with noble views on both sides. *For the most part, our track lay through corn-fields, or skirting small forests. I chatted half the way about Guy Mannering, for it happened that Keats had not then read that novel, and I enjoyed the recollection of the events as I described them in their own scenes. There was a little spot, close to our pathway, where, without a shadow of doubt, old Meg Merrilees had often boiled her kettle, and, haply, cooked a chicken. It was among fragments of rock, and brambles, and broom, and most tastefully ornamented with a profusion of honeysuckle, wild roses, and fox-glove, all in the very blush and fullness of blossom.* The conversation and the scenery inspired Keats to write a poem of four verses in length on Meg Merrilees. Keats dismissed it as a trifle but Brown considered it a good description of Meg. The second verse is worth quoting:

> *Her brothers were the craggy hills*
> *Her sisters larchen trees;*
> *Alone with her great family*
> *She lived as she did please.*
> *No breakfast had she many a morn,*
> *No dinner many a noon,*
> *And, 'stead of supper, she would stare*
> *Full hard against the moon!*

From Auchencairn they headed towards Kirkcudbright passing through Dundrennan to see the Abbey. Brown recorded: *It is the ruin of a stately building, and must have bordered on the magnificent in its original state. Trees were not only growing about, but on the walls. There was, especially, a flourishing ash, that did not*

*Dundrennan Abbey, c.1820 from Johnson's Map of Kirkcudbrightshire, 1821.*

*appear to derive any nourishment from earth; the root spreading itself down the wall, curving its branches between the stones, some forty feet from the ground, and feeding, as far as we could judge, on the mortar alone.*

From Dundrennan the travellers proceeded to Kirkcudbright. *With the town not far before us we were enchanted with the view; the winding bay - the wood-covered hills - the blue mountains beyond them - the island at the mouth of the bay - the sea on each side of it, and in the distance - the extraordinary fertility of the valley, and the surrounding country - all formed a scene that even Keats conferred to be equal and similar to the best parts of his favourite Devon. As we nearer approached the town, through the valley, everything was in a most luxuriant state, the trees, the corn, the verdure and even the hedges - nothing could surpass them.* They also visited the ruins of the Castle but disliked the architecture.

The travellers walked on to Gatehouse of Fleet, admiring Fleet Bay, and then took the coastal road to Creetown. *We soon met, returning to Gate House, men, women and children, of all ages and descriptions. It looked like an emigration, and we inquired the reason; when "The salt water" was the reply, and truly the greater proportion of the population had taken the opportunity of high tide to wash and be clean, where a jutting rock on the coast separated the sexes; and, moreover, they told us it was their daily custom.*

*Gatehouse of Fleet, c.1840.*

After Creetown they went to Newton Stewart, Glenluce, Stranraer, crossed to Ireland from Portpatrick for a few days, and on their return to Scotland walked north through Ayrshire to Glasgow and then into the Highlands. They visited Iona and Staffa and climbed Ben Nevis. On 6th August they reached Inverness and took a coach to Cromarty. From there they sailed back to London.

**NOTES**

1   Meg Merrilees is a character in Sir Walter Scott's 'Guy Mannering' (1815).

# ROBERT SOUTHEY

In the early autumn of 1819 yet another English poet and writer visited Scotland, following the journeys of Dorothy and William Wordsworth, Coleridge and Keats. He was Robert Southey (1774-1843). Southey is probably best known for his ballads such as 'The Inchcape Rock' and 'The Battle of Blenheim.' One of his many books was 'The Lives and Works of the Uneducated Poets' which contains a long chapter on John Taylor the Water-Poet. Southey was accompanied by Thomas Telford, the great Scottish engineer. They had been brought together for the tour through a common friend, John Rickman, who accompanied them.

The tour was a journey of pleasure for Southey, but for Telford it was primarily a tour of inspection of various works in progress, and these to a large extent decided the route. From Carlisle they went through Langholm, Hawick, Edinburgh, Stirling, Aberdeen and Inverness to Loch Alsh and south past Loch Ness to Inveraray, Glasgow and New Lanark and then to Moffat. Southey was a perceptive and interested traveller, who was critical of what rightly offended his standards. His Journal of the tour is a valuable account of what he saw. Unfortunately, like so many visitors, he only passed through the south-west and did not take time to explore it properly.

The relevant passages of his Journal follow: *September 29 - After breakfast 15 miles to Elvan Foot, in part thro' a country almost as dreary and quite as desolate as the Highlands, tho' not so black; the latter part green, hilly and pastoral, resembling the Eskdale country. 13 to Moffat, for the most part on a descent, with the Annan frequently near us.*

> *Tweed, Annan and Clyde*
> *All rise upon one hill's side*
> *Tweed run, Annan won,*
> *Clyde fell and broke his neck.*

*- such is the broken rhyme of the country, as repeated to me by Mr. Telford, himself a native of Langholm. We had gone up the Clyde, and now went down the Annan. Moffat is a pretty little town, frequented at certain seasons because of some mineral waters in the neighbourhood. The surrounding country is monotonous and pastoral.*

*September 30 - the coach was discharged at Moffat, and we proceeded in two post-*

*chaises, starting at seven, so that we got to Lockerbie, 16 miles, to breakfast, meaning to reach Carlisle this night. 20 to Longtown. I turned aside with T. and R. to look at the foundations for an iron bridge over the Esk, upon the new road. The piers are now just above water.*

# WILLIAM COBBETT

*William Cobbett*

Cobbett (1763-1835) was an outspoken English radical politician and writer who championed the plight of the poor. Perhaps he is best known for the account he gave of southern England in 'Rural Rides,' which he published in 1830. He visited Scotland in the autumn of 1832 and his book 'Tour in Scotland' was published in the following January. He was not over-sensitive in his feelings but he had a good grasp of facts.

In early October 1832 he went from Northumberland to Edinburgh, crossed over the Forth to visit Dunfermline, and then went over to the west by Kincardine and Falkirk. After visiting Glasgow and Greenock and New Lanark he travelled south through Ayrshire and Nithsdale to Dumfries which he reached at 5 p.m. on 6 November. At 7.30 p.m. he gave a lecture in the Theatre. Unfortunately he did not record his impression of the town. He stayed the night in Dumfries and left the next morning for Annan, where he gave a lecture at noon. He arrived in Carlisle later on the 7th. His visit to Scotland was therefore brief but long enough for him to shed his prejudices and false notions about the Scots and to admit that they were worthy of highest esteem and warmest affection.

Cobbett's allusion to Dr. Samuel Johnson in the following extract is related to Johnson's visit to Scotland in 1773 in the company of James Boswell. Johnson was scathing about the lack of trees, at least in those parts of Scotland which he saw. He asserted that a tree might be a show in Scotland as a horse in Venice, and that Mr. Boswell found only one at St. Andrews.

The relevant passages of Cobbett's book are as follows:

*Nithsdale, c.1840.*

*Dumfriesshire is much about like Ayrshire in point of land and productions, it is hilly occasionally, and has some fine farms on the flats, some of which are large; but generally they are small; the cottages numerous, built of stone, and made white by whitewashing, which gives a very pretty appearance to the country, though there are, generally speaking, very few trees. We cross several pretty rivers; the orchards are by no means bad, and the apple-trees very clean, the land is moory, and affords peat in several instances, a large part of the land is in pasture; dairy work and the fattening of hogs seem to be the principal uses of the land. The hogs are of the white lop-eared breed. Hams, bacon and butter, are the principal products of the county. The woods are very fine in some parts, especially from Sanquhar to Thornhill, which consists, in great part, of the estate of the Duke of Buccleuch. I suppose that Dr. Johnson did not travel this way, for here is a beautiful river, and immense woods on both sides of it for nine or ten miles at the least; this river, which is called the Nith, goes all the way to the town of Dumfries; and after dividing Dumfriesshire from Kirkcudbrightshire for a few miles, falls into the Solway Firth. Leaving at a great distance to my left the lofty hills, celebrated by Burns, now crowned with snow, while the valleys below are covered with grass and dairies of fine cows, I got on to the town of Dumfries.*

*From Dumfries to the town of Annan (sixteen miles), is a very fine farming country; here and there a peat-moor, with large stacks of peat, that being the fuel of the country, and it being exceedingly good fuel, a man telling me that it boiled a pot quicker than coals, and produced less ashes. Here the cattle are of the Galloway breed, and the dairies are very numerous. Fine large valleys of corn-fields; hanging woods on the sides of the hills like those of Surrey; sometimes hills consisting part of furze, and partly of broom, with a good deal of grassland between them; the cottages very numerous, and the people, particularly the children, looking very well. At eight miles from Dumfries, the Solway Firth, with the sun shining beautifully upon it, presents itself to our right.'* (Cobbett then makes a passionate denunciation of landowners' claims to the absolute right to exclusive proprietorship of land).

*'We have now fine land and fine farming, fine dairies and everything else fine, with here and there a piece of moor and peatland, all the way to the river that divides Cumberland from the county of Dumfries. At Annan we were very hospitably received, and met several gentlemen of the town, at breakfast, at the house of Mr. Nelson. At noon I lectured at the Assembly Room to a very respectable audience, and thus took my farewell of lecturing in Scotland. At the end of ten miles, or thereabouts, we pass over the River Esk, over a very fine bridge, into Cumberland, having about seven miles still to go to reach Carlisle.*(1)

### NOTES

1    An article by Norman and Margaret Miller in the Transactions of the Dumfriesshire and Galloway Natural History and Antiquarian Society, vol. LXVII (1992) gives an account of the construction of the bridge.

# LORD COCKBURN

*Lord Cockburn.*

Henry Thomas Cockburn (1779-1854) was an advocate who became Solicitor-General for Scotland in 1830. Then in 1834 he was appointed a Judge and he assumed the title of Lord Cockburn. He wrote two well-known books which were not published until after his death: "Memorials of his Time" and "Circuit Journeys." The latter is in the form of a diary and records what he saw in Scotland during his Circuits as a Judge from 1837 to 1854. He travelled widely through Scotland covering from the Solway to Inverness and from Iona to St. Andrews. He used various forms of transport: horse-drawn carriages, steamers and railway trains. In 1847 when he was at Dumfries he reflected that *those who are born to railroads, or even to modern mail-coaches, can scarcely be made to understand how we, of the previous age, got on.* He observed that when travelling from Edinburgh in the past *Dumfries and Ayr were both unattainable in one day; and Inveraray was out of the world. Even Glasgow was a good day's work.*

Cockburn was very concerned about the state of ruined abbeys in various parts of Scotland including Galloway. In September 1839 he stopped at New Abbey to see Sweetheart Abbey. *It is a beautiful and venerable fragment. The chief value of this abbey, however, consists in its standing as a monument of the brutality of Scotland in these matters. It is only about twenty-five years ago that the whole pile was not only sold, but was bought actually for the purpose of being taken down and made into stone dykes! And this purpose was partly carried into effect. The liberality (combined, I hope with the indignation) of six or eight gentlemen saved the residue of the ruin by repurchasing it.*(1)

A few days later Cockburn visited Dundrennan Abbey, and again he was indignant about its condition: *Though greatly abridged, it is still a beautiful and interesting mass. But every other feeling is superseded by one's horror and indignation at* the state in which it is kept. If it had been an odious and offensive building, which the Crown and the adjoining landowners were trying to obliterate as fast as possible, and to render disgusting and inaccessible in the meantime, what else could they do? Fortunately the position soon changed. In 1844 he revisited the Abbey and claimed *the principal merit of its being in the state it now is*. As a result of his representations *the Commissioners of Woods and Forests have cleaned out the rubbish, and drained the ground, and made some judicious repairs.*(2)

Cockburn was impressed by Dumfries. In 1844 he wrote: *My love of Dumfries - at least of its beauty - increases. A most respectable country town, it wants nothing but an old cathedral. However, its church and churchyard, its size, half-Anglified, reddish houses, with their bright windows, its clean streets, paved with small stones, its most beautiful river and green, and the memory of Burns, give it all a pleasing and respectable air. I am not sure that there is a more perfectly beautiful village scene anywhere - even on the North Inch(3) - than on looking up the water from the lower end of the green. The spectator must be so far down the green as to lose all the paltry part of Maxwelltown,(4) and to see only Dumfries, lined by the Nith, softened by a few trees, and the prospect bounded by the bridge. Notwithstanding a few black coal sloops, and the pretty constant din of a cursed manufacturing mill at the lower end of the green, it is a singularly serene and pleasing prospect.*

*Kirkcudbright, c.1840.*

Cockburn also admired Kirkcudbright - at least at high tide! In 1839 he wrote: *The prospect from Tongueland Hill is beautiful and peculiar. Kirkcudbright stands like a little Venice, in the midst of its surrounding water.* When Cockburn was in the vicinity of Kirkcudbright, he usually stayed at Cumstoun, just over a mile to the north. In September 1844 he went from there again to Tongueland Hill to have another view of Kirkcudbright: *I doubt if there be a more picturesque country town in Scotland. Small, clean, silent, and respectable; it seems (subject, however, to one enormous deduction) the type of a place to which decent characters and moderate purses would retire for quiet comfort. The deduction arises from the dismal swamps of deep, sleechy(5) mud, by which it is nearly surrounded at low tide. It is only at full tide, or nearly so, that Kirkcudbright is to be viewed therefore, or at such a distance that the difference between water and watery mud is lost. And then, how beautifully does it stand! With its brown ruin of a castle, its church spire, the spire of its old town-house, and the square tower of its new one, all seen above its edging of trees, and the whole village surrounded by wooded hills and apparently glittering sea.*

The south-west of Scotland contains many monuments commemorating the deaths of Covenanters especially in the 1680s who would not surrender their deep religious convictions to conform to the Episcopal Church. While Cockburn was at Cumstoun in September 1844 he went to visit the granite obelisk erected on Kirkconnell moor in 1831 in memory of the shooting by Grierson of Lagg in 1685 of five covenanters (John Bell, James Clement, David Halliday, Robert Lennox and Andrew McRobert) despite having been given quarter by Colonel Douglas.

Cockburn recorded: *The funds for the erection of this testimony were produced by a sermon preached on the spot upon the 11th of September 1831, to which, notwithstanding the month and the elevation, about 10,000 people listened.* This remarkable event shows the continuing strength of religious fervour at that time in Galloway.

Cockburn then went on *an expedition to the lighthouse on the island of Little Ross, about six or seven miles below Kirkcudbright(6). Some rode and some drove, and George Maitland walked till we all came to the alehouse on the peninsula of Great Ross, where we took boat, and after about a mile's sailing, were landed on the island. It is one of the lesser lights. All its machinery was explained to us by a sensible keeper. I never understood the thing before. The prospect from the top, and, indeed from every part of the island, is beautiful.* On the following day Cockburn went in a leaky boat with bad oars from Kirkcudbright to a place about six miles below, on the east side of the bay, called Dirk Hatteraick's Cave(7)… *the said cave is perfect nonsense. A narrow, wet, dirty slit in a rock, produced by the washing away of the loose matter between two vertically laminated rocks, and answering Scott's scenery in no one respect.*


## NOTES

1   Much of the Abbey Church (though not its roof) has survived due to a local consortium purchasing it in 1779 with the intention of preserving it.

2   The Abbey had been plundered for its stones during the 17th century and much of the 18th. In 1838 Lord Selkirk began the clearance of debris and some other repairs at his own expense. The Commissioners in 1841 authorised the commencement of more repairs. This saved what was left of the Abbey for several decades. Early in the 20th century further work was carried out each summer.

3   The North Inch is in Perth adjacent to the River Tay.

4   Maxwelltown is part of Dumfries on the west side of the River Nith. It was a separate burgh until 1929.

5   Slimy.

6   R. L. Stevenson's father built the lighthouse on the Little Ross. Stevenson's novel The Master of Ballantrae is set not at Ballantrae in Ayrshire but in the location of Borgue between Kirkcudbright and Gatehouse of Fleet.

7   This cave is near Torrs Point in Kirkcudbright Bay and is now within the M.O.D. range. Dirk Hatteraick was a fictional character in Sir Walter Scott's 'Guy Mannering.' He was a smuggler who landed his cargoes on the Galloway coast. Scott in his subsequent Notes to the novel stated that there was a cave near the old Castle of Raeberry about six miles below Kirkcudbright which was being called Dirk Hatteraick's cave. The site of the former Raeberry Castle, however, is about 2 miles along the coast to the east of the cave and is also within the M.O.D. range. There is another cave called Dirk Hatteraick's on the shore between Cardoness and Carsluith near Barholm Castle. This cave is described in detail by C. H. Dick in his 'Highways and Byways in Galloway and Carrick.' He commented that it did not correspond with the cave in the novel in any particular.

# JAMES WILSON

The Zoologist James Wilson was born at Paisley in 1795 and went to school in Edinburgh. Starting in 1816 he travelled on the continent and also resided for a time in Italy. From 1824 he lived near Edinburgh and devoted himself to his scientific and literary interests. In the summer of 1841 he accompanied the Secretary to the Commissioners of the Board of Fisheries on a voyage round the coast of Scotland. The purpose was to study the natural history of the herring and make other observations of interest to the fishing industry. They sailed on a Fisheries Service Cutter of 103 tons from Greenock, and visited many places not within the range of the ordinary tourist. In 1854 he was offered but declined the chair of Natural History in Edinburgh University. He died in 1856. Wilson wrote several books including 'A Voyage round the Coasts of Scotland' about his voyage in 1841. The following passages are from that account.

After a stormy night they cast anchor in the mouth of Loch Ryan and at 4 a.m. on 22 June after obtaining a pilot they arrived at Stranraer:

*Many kinds of white fish are found in this far-stretching island bay, but for many years back it has been almost entirely forsaken by herring. Yet it was at one time famous for that fish. The clergyman of the parish observes, "I have heard old people say that they have known 300 sail-boats in the bay at one time, which had come from the Highlands and other places, in order to fish or purchase herrings." Indeed, even the white fish have decreased in quantity, and haddocks especially, which about 30 years ago were good and plentiful, are now of rare occurrence. Excellent oysters are found on a sandy bank called the Scar, which projects from a promontory of the western shore. There is a good deal of cultivation on both sides, but little wood…. Numerous waterfowl occur in this district, and we observed a Merlin (a rare breeding bird in Scotland) fly from the second story of an old silver-fir on the peninsular portion of the Castle (Kennedy) grounds. The larger beasts of prey, such as foxes, wild-cats, and badgers, are said to have entirely disappeared, although the polecat and weasel are still well known.*

*We drove one morning with Colonel Blair, (a Waterloo officer, who had just returned from the agreeable and gratifying duty of dining with the Duke, on the anniversary of the great day,) as far as his estate of Dunskey, near Portpatrick. We proceeded on foot to inspect the grounds. We were certainly surprised when first informed that scarcely a tree existed here five-and twenty years ago, except a few planted by the late Sir James Hunter Blair; and now, notwithstanding its vicinity to a bold and rocky shore, and unscreened exposure to the ocean blasts, there are from four to five hundred acres of excellent and even vigorous plantations. But, as the Secretary pointed out, with his accustomed perception of both the useful and the picturesque, a great advantage is gained by the ground being, though high, yet varied by numerous deep and sheltering hollows, between the prevailing elevated ranges.*

*In relation to the general fisheries of this portion of the coast, it may be observed that the capture of herrings has been abandoned since the withdrawal of the bounty(1). From 1813 to 1821, about 20 boats and 100 men were employed in the Portpatrick herring fishery, each boat using from 1200 to 1600 yards of net, and averaging a profit of £80. The greater number of these fish were caught between Portpatrick and Portnessock, at a distance of from two to three miles from shore, and the usual fishing season was midsummer, from the commencement of June to the beginning of August. It was the prevailing belief that they then proceeded southwards to the Isle of Man, where the fishery began about the 10th of August. In those days 120 herring boats, assembled from different quarters, have been seen together in Portpatrick harbour. As soon as the herring fishery was discontinued, that for cod commenced upon a systematic plan, and was chiefly carried on from November to the end of March.*

*It need scarcely be observed that steam navigation has been of essential service to Wigtownshire in general. That mode of communication now exists between her principal ports and Liverpool and Whitehaven, in addition to the intercourse with Glasgow and Stranraer. These open a quick and ready market both for grain and livestock, and for ready money, at the current prices; whereas, in former times, sales were scarcely ever met by cash. Travelling corn-dealers bought up the grain (by bills) with a view of shipment to the English market, and being seldom men of capital, and their trade precarious, a greater proportion became bankrupt than in almost any other class. Those who purchased cattle, to drive for sale to England, were much in the same predicament, and likewise paid by means of bills. Hence the Wigtownshire farmers were frequently exposed to risk, and not seldom suffered the severest losses. But steam navigation has entirely changed the condition of affairs. At the same time, as no human invention is perfect in all its relative consequences, some counteracting disadvantages have since ensued. Portpatrick is no longer the entrance to the highway from Ireland to England, the steamers plying direct to Liverpool or Holyhead. The importation both of black cattle and horses has also much diminished.*

**NOTE**

1  In 1749 an Act of Parliament introduced a bounty system to encourage the herring industry against competition from the Dutch. As a result of the Napoleonic War the Dutch fishing fleet declined and after 1829 the bounty system was terminated.

# WILLIAMU

In 1860 the Rev. John and Mrs. Inglis returned to Scotland from their missionary work in the New Hebrides, which are in the south-west of the Pacific Ocean. They brought with them from the island of Aneityum a Christian convert called Williamu. The Christian Gospel had been introduced by Samoan teachers to Aneityum in 1841. Williamu who was about 14 years old at that time, attached himself to the missionaries despite threats and blows from other islanders. The name Williamu was given to him by the Samoans from the name of the famous missionary John Williams who had been killed in 1839 while trying to land on one of the islands.

Williamu was impressed with the remarkable kindness and goodness of the people whom he met in Britain and also by the abundance of food. At first he was chary of eating too much as he thought the food provisions would soon be consumed. In winter he was perplexed by the low position of the sun in the sky, as on Aneityum the sun is high in the sky at mid-day even on the shortest days.

Williamu stayed in Britain for 2½ years and wrote many letters to relatives in Aneityum and friends in Britain. Mr. Inglis translated some of these letters into English and kept copies. The letters were unaided compositions and revealed Williamu's impressions of life in Britain.

He returned to Aneityum where he died in 1878. He was described as kind, unselfish and generous. His letters are contained in a book written by John Inglis when living at Lincuan Cottage, Kirkcowan in Wigtownshire in 1889. Most of Williamu's published letters were written while he was staying with Mr. and Mrs. Inglis at Newton Stewart.

Letter to his wife Dora from Newton Stewart on 4 January, 1861:

*When we arrived here in June, it was not cold. But the cold began in October, and snow fell, but it was not much. The water also was frozen and became hard, only it was but little. But when November came the cold was very severe, and a great deal of snow fell and covered all the ground. You could not see any growing thing. It was as if you had spread out white clothes and covered both the ground and the houses with them. But it was very beautiful and very white. You could just see the trees and the houses and the fences. The frost came down and the water was hard. What Mr. and Mrs. Inglis told us is quite true, that the water becomes hard, and when the people go to get water they have to break it like glass, and then get water. Very great is the cold in Britain in November, December and January. Your hands get benumbed, and you can do nothing with them.*

Letter to his half-brother Mathima from Newton Stewart on 29 January 1861 (He is referring to the house which Mr. and Mrs. Inglis were renting):

*It is a very good house. There are a great many rooms in it. There are five apartments below and three above. The walls are smooth and beautiful, and covered with painted paper. Moreover, it is fitted up with lights which they call gas. This gas is first made out of coal, and kept in a vessel like a very large cask, and then it goes under the ground in large iron pipes; it goes like wind; then it comes up into the houses and stays there always and when it becomes dark then they light it every night.*

Letter to Mrs. Snodgrass at Castle Douglas dated 20 September 1860:

*Castle Douglas from Carlingwark Hill, c.1875 from: Maxwell's Guide to the Stewartry of Kirkcudbright, 1st edition.*

*When I came here with Mr. and Mrs. Inglis, and saw this country, I had no words to express my wonder and my joy. There are such crowds of people here; the houses are all built close to one another; the land is everywhere so well cultivated, and the conduct of the people is so good; they all speak so lovingly to one another and live in such peace. Truly this is not the way that we lived among ourselves on the other side of the world.*

Letter to his wife Dora on Aneityum dated 20 August 1860 (Mr. and Mrs. Inglis had taken Williamu to visit Edinburgh. On their return journey they stayed for a night at Kilmarnock and next morning went by train to Thornhill):

*We alighted at a village called Thornhill, and travelled in a thing drawn by a horse till we came to the village in which Mr. Inglis was born; its name is Moniaive. This was as far as from Aname to Anelgauhat. When we came there we stayed in the house of Mr. Proudfoot. Both he and his wife are very kind people. They were both very good to me. On the Friday there was a marriage there, and Mr. Proudfoot and I went to see it. On the Sabbath day all the people were very desirous to hear Mr. Inglis. I had to rise and go out of the church; my former illness, fever and ague, came upon me. First my legs were benumbed and then my hands. Mrs. Inglis and I went into the church, but she brought me back into the house. My illness, however, was not great, and it has now quite left me. On the next day, the Monday, we three came to the house of Mrs. Inglis's sister, Mr. McGeoch, Craignell, near New Galloway. This was as far from Iteng to Itheg.*

Letter to his cousin Sabataio from Newton Stewart dated 1 April 1861. (Williamu is referring to the opening of the railway-line between Castle Douglas and Stranraer): *They have finished the road here for the things that run by smoke. It was opened in March. The great men who are the owners of it travelled along it first. I went to see them. All the people were assembled. There might be a thousand people there. The running is far faster than that of a horse. The road is as far as from Aneityum to Efate.* (Efate is another island in the New Hebrides and the comparison in distance was sound).

Letter to his Uncle Talep from Newton Stewart dated 10 September 1861:

*Britain is a remarkable country for religion, and for the kindness of the people to one another and to strangers. The people all go to church every Sabbath day without ceasing, and they often meet also on week days. Into whatever house I go, the people are all so kind to me, and seem so glad to see me.*

Letter also to Talep from Newton Stewart on 25 March 1862:

*I had a cough, and Mr. Inglis was afraid of me, and gave me medicine, and took care of me, and made me stay in the house, and made me put on more clothes in the daytime, and gave me more blankets at night, and I live as they do. In the same way all the people are good to me here in this great land. Such is their way in this land of light. They treat me as if I had been born here, and as if I were the child of everybody in the land, their kindness to me is so great and their treatment of me is so good. They are not kind to me because I am a chief, or for anything they see about me. It is just the way they do in this land of light, from the grace of God in their hearts. I speak, and Mr. Inglis interprets in English what I say. I have spoken in eight churches, and explained our heathen customs that we clung to long ago. I spoke before great crowds, as many as are assembled on Aneityum at the time of the communions. The churches were full.*

# GEORGE BORROW

GEORGE BORROW

*George Borrow*

George Borrow (1803-81) was an English author and traveller. He decided to leave his work in London as a hack-writer to become a tramp. This brought him into contact with gipsies, leading to his books on scenes of gipsy life. Subsequently he travelled in Russia, Spain, Portugal and Morocco. He was one of the most remarkable and eccentric individuals of his time. His works include The Bible in Spain (1843), Lavengro (1851), The Romany Rye (1857) and Wild Wales (1862).

In 1858 he toured the Scottish Highlands, visiting Oban, Iona, Kintyre, Inverness and Wick and also Orkney and Shetland. Then in 1866 he crossed from Ulster to Stranraer to walk through Galloway and the Scottish Borders. Apart from his itinerary, he recorded few impressions, but some of his notes are worth quoting.

On 18 July he left Stranraer and headed for Glen Luce. *Set off in the direction of Castle Stewart. Fine view of mountans on the left. Plantations and old Castle in the foreground. Most beautiful scene I ever saw - hot sun - far distant misty mountains - cattle in the water - stay and look at them. Discourse with a Scotch pedlar - been everywhere - Dunragit and Delragit - Glen Luce. Regular old-fashioned Scottish town - very beautfiul scenery, hills and wood. McLellan's hotel. Ale. Stroll about the town. The glen - the little bridge - the rivulet and the trees - children playing in the water - strong smell of turf-smoke throughout the village. Capital dinner. Cool delightful evening. People in the streets sitting or standing, enjoying the cool. Return to the inn. Sleep comfortably.*

19 July at Glenluce: *Go to the sea to bathe - two miles distant - coast rocky - some difficulty in getting down to the water - some people bathing - none could swim - seemed surprised that I could. Go to Crow's Nest(1), a house by the sea side. Visit Abbey on New Luce road - belongs to Sir John Hay of Castle Park. Return. The miller and his friends seated on a stone wall drinking cool water out of a basin - discourse about the war* (Borrow was referring to the war between Prussia and Austria) *and the Pope of Rome. Many Papists in the neighbourhood, but all Irish - the natives all Protestants.*

*Glenluce Abbey, Interior of the Chapter House from "Archaeological and Historical Collections relating to Ayrshire and Galloway" vo. V, 1885.*

*Dinner: rice soup, salmon, mutton chop, pancake. Stroll. Free Church - minister preaching in a meadow near the bridge.*

On 20 July Borrow left Glen Luce for Newton Stewart: *Proceeded for several miles between hills, the sun was burning hot - in fact, I never was out in a fiercer summer day. The land seemed to be very poor and sterile. Saw at last a kind of lake(2), on my right apparently about three hundred yards across. A cottage stood near it, and seeing a woman engaged in weeding a potato garden, I entered into conversation with her. We first talked about the weather, and she told me that the crops had suffered much from drought. I praised the country, but she did not agree with me, saying that it was a 'coorse country'. She spoke in the broadest Galloway dialect, and I had the greatest difficulty in understanding what she said. I asked her the name of the place where we were, the lake, and the distant hills. She said, Carn Top, Dushelwyn(3) Loch, and Cairnsmore. That there were fish in the loch, but not many. "Are they pike?" I asked. "Geddes"(4), she replied. Proceed. Came to a toll-bar kept by one John Douglas, a little short fellow of seventy-three. Wretched country. Kirkcowan on the right. Took wrong road. Written under the shade of trees, sitting on a stone near a house, after passing over the dreadful sunburnt moors. No water - at length came to a pleasant valley - asked a girl if there was any water near. She said that there was none that she knew of. Presently saw a little rill under some trees. Sat down. The horse and cart with the women and children. "Will it please you, Sir, to raise in order that the mare may go down to drink." When they were gone I drank and drank. Newton Stewart, Black's Hotel.*

Borrow proceeded eastward to Dumfries and Carlisle. On 30 July he went from Carlisle to Langholm: *eight miles to Langholm - night descending fast - push on up steep hill - told by lads that there was a wild bull farther on - at the end of about a mile and a half saw a large dark object in a field to the right - the bull - he said nothing to me nor I to him - reached Langholm somewhat after ten at night. Crown Inn - landlord tenant to the Duke of Buccleuch.* From Langholm he went across to Hawick and Berwick. There he took the train to Edinburgh and Glasgow and then returned to Belfast by steamer.

**NOTES**

1 Stairhaven.

2 Barhapple Loch.

3 Derskelpin, the name of the nearby farm.

4 Ged is Scots for a pike.

# JOHN RUSKIN

*John Ruskin*

Ruskin, writer and critic, was born in London in 1819. His Scottish ancestry included the Agnews of Lochnaw, the Adairs of Genoch, and the Ross family (which included Sir John Ross the Arctic explorer) of Balsarroch in Kirkcolm Parish, all in Wigtownshire. Some members of his family were living in Galloway. Ruskin wrote and lectured on various subjects, especially Art and Social Morals. In 1869 he was elected a Professor of Art in Oxford University. His views on standards for aesthetic subjects were very influential. Although his health began to deteriorate from 1878, he managed to write "Praeterita" which contained recollections of his own life. He died in 1900.

In "Praeterita" he stressed the contribution of the pastoral country from Annan to the Mull of Galloway in forming the highest intellectual and moral powers of the Scots. In 1876 he stayed at Kenmure Castle. In "Praeterita" he recalled trying there *to recollect on what height above Solway, Darsie Latimer pauses with Wandering Willie, in whom Scott records for ever the glory, - not of Scottish music only, but of all Music, rightly so called, - which is a part of God's own creation, becoming an expression of the purest hearts. I cannot pause now to find the spot, and still less the churchyard in which, at the end of Wandering Willie's Tale, his grandsire wakes: but, to the living reader, I have this to say very earnestly, that the whole glory and blessing of these sacred coasts depended on the rise and fall of their eternal sea, over sands which the sunset gilded with its withdrawing glow, from the measureless distances of the west, on the ocean horizon, or veiled in silvery mists, or shadowed with fast-flying storm, of which nevertheless every cloud was pure, and the winter snows blanched in the starlight. For myself, the impressions of the Solway sands are a part of the greatest teaching that ever I received during the joy of youth.*

Although Ruskin had much to say about Scott's Redgauntlet and also Old Mortality, he recorded little else about his own impressions of the Solway, but at least he drew attention to the beauty of the Solway sands. In certain lights these can be spectacular when the tide is out.

# THE 20TH CENTURY

In the course of the 20th century the pace of life accelerated very markedly and significantly. Travelling became much faster and easier with the arrival of motor vehicles, aeroplanes and fast ocean liners followed by jumbo jets. Travel abroad was accessible to vast numbers of people instead of the favoured few, and holidays within Britain were less fashionable.

In the first half of the century the cinema was immensely popular, but subsequently it lost favour with the arrival of TV and then videos. There were pressures for everything to be provided immediately, and no longer was there time just to stand and stare. The art of keeping a diary with long descriptive accounts of visits and journeys became a rare accomplishment. By the end of the century life was increasingly dominated by the ubiquitous microchip, providing immediate access to a massive display of information. It is therefore not surprising that accounts of visits within Britain, including Dumfries and Galloway, became much rarer.

Two outstanding 20th century authors included delightful vignettes of Galloway scenery and activities in their books. Dorothy L. Sayers enjoyed holidays in Kirkcudbright. In 'The Five Red Herrings' (1931) there are descriptions of contemporary life in Kirkcudbright and Gatehouse of Fleet and also of the scenery at Gatehouse of Fleet station and along the road from Gatehouse to Creetown. John Buchan stayed at Ardwall near Gatehouse when he was on holiday as an Oxford undergraduate in the late 1890s. His exploration of nearby Galloway countryside is reflected in novels such as 'The Thirty-Nine Steps' and 'Castle Gay' and also in several short stories. (It must be stressed that the Scottish part of 'The Thirty-Nine Steps' took place mainly in Galloway and not in the Highlands as shown in the film versions). In his memoirs 'Memory Hold-The-Door' (1940) he recounted: *Once I walked sixty-three miles on end in the Galloway Hills. It was my custom in the long vacations to bury myself in the moorlands, taking up my quarters in a shepherd's cottage. There I rose early, worked for five or six hours, and then went fishing until the summer midnight. I throve on a diet of oatmeal, mutton and strong tea. At that time the Mecca of sport for us was the house of Ardwall in Kirkcudbrightshire, the home of Lord Ardwall, the last of the great "characters" on the Scottish Bench and a figure who might have stepped out of a Raeburn canvas. There between the hills and the sea a party of us forgathered each autumn. Those were royal days when we rode and walked and shot all over Galloway as far as the Dungeon of Buchan, and returned in the small hours of the morning to prodigious feasts. Looking back it is hard to see how we escaped with our lives, for we would hunt the hare on horseback with greyhounds among the briers and bogs and boulders of a Galloway moor, and swim our horses over the estuary of the Fleet at high tide. We almost came to believe that our necks were spared for the judicial end which Lord Ardwall always predicted.*

At the end of May 1940 Norwegian soldiers, who had escaped from Norway after its seizure by the Germans arrived in Dumfries. They had lost everything except the clothes they wore. They were joined by several hundred Norwegian whalers who had been in the Antarctic. Their numbers gradually increased as more Norwegians escaped from Norway, and at one time over 1000 men and over 100 girls were in training. The Norwegians were popular visitors and they entered into the life of Dumfries, rapidly learning the language, attending Burns Suppers, and playing football against Queen of the South. Their canteen, called Norway House, was in Church Place opposite the Burns Statute.

They also used several other buildings in Dumfries and outside the town such as Goldielea House (off the A711); Mouswald Place, Mouswald; Craigdarroch near Moniaive and Newlands (where they had their hospital) to the east of Dalswinton. Dumfries with its tidal river reminded many of the Norwegians of their own towns and countryside. There continue to be close links between Dumfries and Norway.

On 15 March 1972 there was a memorable day in Langholm when Neil Armstrong, who in 1969 had been the first man to step on the moon, became the first Freeman of the 'Muckle Toon'. There was bright sunshine on that day and the Armstrongs accompanied by the Provost and his wife were able to travel in an open landau preceded by the Langholm Pipe Band from the Town Hall to Langholm's Old Parish Church where the Freedom Ceremony took place. Armstrong, whose ancestors came from Eskdale, promised to defend the liberties of the Burgh of Langholm in all time coming. In reply to the Provost's address he said: *the most difficult place to be recognised is in one's home town – I consider this Langholm to be my home town. I have gained a new home today. I feel very comfortable here – Langholm people are my kind of people, and while this is my first trip to Langholm, I hope it will not be my last.* He also referred to the unique honour which had been conferred on him. After the luncheon in the Buccleuch Halls Armstrong said he was most impressed with the warmth of the welcome he had received in Langholm, and that he was proud indeed to be Langholm's First Freeman.

# INDEX TO VISITORS AND TO SOME PLACES MENTIONED IN THEIR NARRATIVES

### BOLD LETTERS ARE VISITORS; BOLD NUMBERS ARE ILLUSTRATIONS

*To See Oursels...*